CARING

DENISE MASSEY

CARING

Six Steps for
Effective Pastoral Conversations

Abingdon Press
Nashville

CARING:
SIX STEPS FOR EFFECTIVE PASTORAL CONVERSATIONS

Copyright © 2019 Denise Massey

ISBN: 9781501884580

Library of Congress Control Number: 2019948258

19 20 21 22 23 24 25 26 27 28 — 10 9 8 7 6 5 4 3 2 1
MANUFACTURED IN THE UNITED STATES OF AMERICA

*This book is lovingly dedicated
to my husband, Charles,
and my sons, Patrick and Christopher,
with heartfelt gratitude for the CARING you have provided for me
as I wrote this book and throughout our lives together.*

I deeply appreciate your support, encouragement, and love.

CONTENTS

Preface   xi

Acknowledgments   xiii

INTRODUCTION   xviii
    Problems Ministers Experience   xviii
    Solutions This Book Offers   xxi
    Coaching as a Resource for Ministers   xxiii
    An Integrated Process (Pastoral Care,
       Spiritual Direction, and Coaching)   xxv
    Overview of the Six Steps (CARING)   xxvi
    Overview of the Book   xxviii
    How to Use This Book   xxxi

CHAPTER ONE, Step 1: Connect with God, Self,
and Others   1
    Your Long-Term Preparation   1
    Your Short-Term Preparation: Before the Conversation   3
    Begin the Conversation (Scheduled Meetings)   12
    Introduce the Process   14
    Guide the Connecting Experience   16
    Begin the Conversation
       (Unscheduled Requests for Help)   18
    Make the Decision   19
    Establish the Agreement   20
    Appropriately Maintain the Agreement   20
    Pitfalls to Avoid   21
    How to Know You Have Completed This Step   23

CHAPTER TWO, Step 2: Attend to the Journey
and Assess the Need   25
    Listen Well   26
    Respond (Let the Other Know You Are Listening)   29
    Begin the Attending Step   30
    Topics to Avoid while Attending   35
    Pitfalls to Avoid while Attending   39
    Assess the Need   40
    Pitfalls to Avoid while Assessing the Need   42
    Integrating Previous Steps and Ongoing Use
      of This Step   43
    How to Know You Have Completed This Step   45

CHAPTER THREE, Step 3: Reach Clarity about
the Realistic Focus for This Conversation   47
    How a Clear Focus Helps   48
    Reach Clarity   49
    How to Develop Good Goals   50
    When the Person Has Difficulty Choosing a Goal   52
    Assess the Chosen Goal   55
    Conclude This Step   58
    Pitfalls to Avoid   58
    Integrating Previous Steps and Ongoing Use
      of This Step   60
    Blending Steps Two and Three   61
    The Hourglass Image   61
    How to Know You Have Completed This Step   62

CHAPTER FOUR, Step 4: Inspire the Development
of a Loving Action Plan   63
    When the Congregant Creates a Plan Immediately
      after Clarifying the Focus   64
    Introduce This Step   66
    Develop an Inspired Action Plan   76
    When Developing an Action Plan Is Difficult   77
    Assess the Plan   80
    Pitfalls to Avoid   80

Integrating Previous Steps and Ongoing Use of
   This Step   82
How to Know You Have Completed This Step   83

CHAPTER FIVE, Step 5: Navigate around Obstacles   85
Introduce and Begin This Step   87
A Conversational Process   87
When There Are Several Obstacles   88
Getting around an Obstacle   90
More In-Depth Help   91
When the Obstacle Is a Thought   92
When the Obstacle Is a Feeling   94
When the Obstacle Is an Action or Inaction   97
Pitfalls to Avoid   99
Integrating Previous Steps and Ongoing Use
   of This Step   100
How to Know You Have Completed This Step   101

CHAPTER SIX, Step 6: Generate Commitment
to a Specific, Loving Action Plan   103
Generate Commitment to a Specific Plan of Action   104
The Importance of Specifics   106
Review the Action Plan   110
Support and Encourage   110
Make a Plan for Accountability   111
Conclude the Conversation   113
Pitfalls to Avoid   114
Integrating Previous Steps and Ongoing Use
   of This Step   115
How to Know You Have Completed This Step   117

CONCLUSION   119
Overview   119
Applications to Ministry   122
Next Steps   123

NOTES   127

PREFACE

For as long as I can remember, I have been one of those people who others seek out to assist with their problems. I found joy in caring for people, which was supported and nurtured in my Protestant church. As a college-bound young person, I experienced a call to pastoral ministry. I remember saying to family and friends that I wished there was a way to do ministry that was mostly helping people with their problems and their spiritual growth. I discovered just such a resource when I attended seminary, completed a PhD in psychology of religion and pastoral care, and received certification as a pastoral educator (called CPE Supervisor at that time) with the Association for Clinical Pastoral Education (ACPE). I have been fascinated by the intricacies of ministry conversations as a pastoral care provider, pastoral educator, and pastoral care professor, teaching courses in psychology of religion, pastoral care, spiritual formation, spiritual care, and emotional intelligence.

Because of the commitment to faculty development by Mercer University School of Theology, where I serve as associate professor of pastoral care and counseling, I received life coach training. I found that adding the skills of coaching—particularly clear focus, accountability, and action plans—complemented the skills I had already developed as a spiritual caregiver. My pastoral conversations became much more effective. I began working on a draft of this book with the working title *The Coaching Minister*. I struggled with writing the book, experiencing many obstacles firsthand. I was chagrined to discover that I could not coach myself to complete my writing project. Then I began to doubt my methodology.

So, I went back to the clinical method of learning, which the Association for Clinical Pastoral Education Standards & Manuals document describes as "an educational model that uses data from the practice of ministry as the content for reflection."[1] In this process, action is followed by reflection that leads to improved action. I always tell my students that the most significant growth occurs when we reflect on ministry situations that did not go well. Practicing what I preach, I began reflecting on what was not successful in the "ministry coaching" methodology I had developed. I discovered that I had left out some important pastoral and spiritual resources, and I had overemphasized some coaching approaches.

I created the six-step process this book describes to correct these imbalances, seeking to integrate pastoral care, spiritual direction, and life coaching. I tested and refined this process in the classroom and with my coaching and spiritual direction clients. You hold in your hands one proof of the effectiveness of the six-step process for effective pastoral conversations. I was able to successfully use the process to support my writing of this book. Many of my students have testified to the effectiveness of this methodology in their ministries. The most important proof will come from your own use of this book's six-step process in your own life and ministry.

ACKNOWLEDGMENTS

Throughout my professional life as a student and teacher of spiritual care, I have been fortunate to learn from numerous people. Professors, supervisors, peers, colleagues, clients, ministers, therapists, spiritual directors, authors, coaches, and students have all contributed to my knowledge and skill. I greatly appreciate each of you.

I completed this manuscript while on sabbatical from my position as associate professor of pastoral care and counseling at Mercer University School of Theology. I am grateful to Mercer University for the sabbatical leave, and I appreciate my colleagues at McAfee School of Theology who protected my research time as much as possible. It is such a gift to have focused time to bring a project to completion. I am truly grateful.

My sincere thanks go to all students and clients who contributed to my thinking about *CARING: Six Steps for Effective Pastoral Conversations.* Doctor of ministry and master of divinity students who have been in my classes "Coaching Individuals, Groups, and Congregations for Spiritual Growth" and "The Coaching Minister" will recognize that they were taught an earlier version of the CARING process, as will many former ACPE students. My theory and process has evolved, and some of the steps have changed over time. Nevertheless, your thinking, practicing pastoral conversations, and questioning influenced the development of this work. To all of the students who asked me, "Will you put that idea in your book?" I hope that you recognize your contributions here!

To the colleagues who helped me think more clearly and write more clearly, I offer my heartfelt thanks. I am deeply appreciative to John Patton for his careful critique and thought-provoking questions about my work. John, co-supervising with you while writing this book was a creative delight. Rochelle Melander and Diane Doulyssi offered invaluable encouragement and nurture for my writing process. I am especially grateful to Nancy Penton, who provided significant editorial and style assistance. Nancy, your competence, pastoral care knowledge, and attention to detail made this a better and more readable book. Along with editorial genius, you also offered remarkable spiritual encouragement and support. Thank you for sharing your gifts with me. Several teaching assistants provided specific help with this manuscript. My sincere appreciation is offered to Noelle Owen, Jaye Peabody, and Hannah Rule. My book is a more helpful guide for ministers because of your participation.

I am grateful to the editorial team at Abingdon Press who nurtured this manuscript to grow into the book you are now reading. An enthusiastic thank-you goes to my editor, Connie Stella, who believed in this project and who capably and compassionately guided me to bring it to completion. I appreciate Erin Pearce, production manager, for capably overseeing the editing and production of this book. Peggy Shearon was invaluable in shepherding the business and logistical aspects of the process. Thank you to the professional staff of Abingdon for supporting the development and publication of this book.

Finally, I offer heartfelt thanks to my family, whose love and support sustained me. My husband, Charles, has provided ongoing care, encouragement, and occasionally the much-needed push! Thank you for all the ways you have shown your support and care. I am truly grateful. Patrick and Christopher, my adult sons, have cheered me on with interest and goodwill. In the early days of my research, they were willing guinea pigs, and I look back on those conversations fondly. Thank you, dear family, for nurturing me as I brought forth this book.

To you, the reader, thank you for picking up this book. Welcome to a journey toward learning more effective ways to guide pastoral conversations. I hope that my written work will become meaningful and real as you make use of this material in your ministry.

INTRODUCTION

Welcome! I imagine that you picked up this book or opened it on your device because you are searching for a better way to care for people. I see you in my mind's eye as a compassionate minister who would like to improve your skills of spiritual and practical care. You may be an experienced minister who regularly faces the difficulties of helping the growing number of persons who come to you for assistance in solving their problems. You might be a beginning minister seeking to develop new knowledge and skills to provide help. All ministers can find value in exploring how to guide people in finding powerful spiritual solutions to their problems.

I am deliberately addressing you, my readers, in a personal way. I intend to offer assistance directly and clearly throughout my book. As a professor and supervisor of spiritual care, I have explored for many years the struggles and the joys of conducting ministry conversations. I am addressing this book to ministers in a variety of roles, including local church pastors, church staff members, chaplains, and ministers in institutions. I will use the terms "parishioner" or "congregant" to refer to the people with whom you minister. If you are a chaplain or other institutional minister, I hope this terminology reminds you that your patients, residents, or clients may be considered your congregation, as you are their pastor. Your helping conversations with people are appropriately called pastoral conversations, whether you are a pastor or serve in another position. In every ministry role, people expect you to be able to help them with their problems, and they will see you as their pastor or spiritual guide.

While I write as a Christian and from the perspective of a Protestant minister, I hope to be welcoming and inclusive of all clergy. I will not try to speak from or to other traditions, but I invite those from other backgrounds to make your own applications and adjustments to my basic framework so that you care for people with personal and theological integrity. My hope is that this work will be broadly applicable.

I believe that love for God, self, and others is the primary theological foundation for pastoral conversations. Helping your parishioners grow toward love is the underlying goal of ministry conversations. I see the problems your congregants bring to you as an indication that they need to experience more love for themselves, other people, and God. From this perspective, problem-solving conversations are a significant opportunity for ministry. Unfortunately, helping your parishioners solve their problems can be the occasion for much struggle and frustration, rather than an opportunity for you to facilitate their transformation. I hope to guide you out of the struggle and frustration and into the joy of conducting pastoral conversations that facilitate spiritual growth.

Problems Ministers Experience

You already know that ministry conversations can be difficult. Some common problems occur regularly. Many times ministers flounder in conversations, not sure what to do or how to help.

Your parishioners turn to you with all kinds of specific and very complicated problems. Additionally, you may have unrealistic expectations for yourself, which are intensified by unrealistic expectations from your congregation or organization. You may experience a lack of time to do everything expected of you. You may feel unclear about how to manage the number of congregants asking for your help. Ministry conversations can be a struggle for all of these reasons, and more.

In my work as a professor and ministry supervisor, I have seen two specific difficulties arise repeatedly, even for seasoned ministers. One is the inability to help parishioners master their fears, doubts, and obstacles. The second is being unclear about where your responsibilities end and your parishioners' responsibilities begin.

Finally, and perhaps most importantly, you may experience a lack of knowledge and skill, feeling that your training did not prepare you for the realities of your ministry. I was once with a group of experienced ministers who were reflecting on this painful situation. One experienced pastor said, "I've never had a class in listening, and I have to admit that I don't really know how to truly hear what my church members are saying." Another commented, "The family systems theory that I learned in seminary didn't really help me know what to do when people ask me for help." A colleague replied, "I learned psychodynamic theories, and I'm not sure what to do when people ask for my help either. It was like trying to apply counseling theories to being a pastor without having learned to be a counselor."

I asked the group, "What do you wish you had been taught?" The answers came quickly and easily. "Listening," said one. "Caring," said another. "Reading between the lines," was the third response. The next person bluntly replied, "Knowing when to keep my mouth shut!" That comment led to startled laughs, rueful looks, and a thoughtful silence. Then the answers went a little deeper. One minister reflected, "I'd like to know how to respond so that people leave feeling like they got something meaningful from me." Another pastor said, "I'd like to know what helps people grow and what gets in their way." He continued quietly, "Sometimes I think I get in their way." Everyone in the circle nodded and smiled with understanding. Then one said, "If I just understood how people really grow and change, I would be a better pastor. My church members want to make changes in their lives, but they don't follow through. And I don't know how to support them."

When the group got quiet, I summarized, "You all want to be able to listen and relate to your people in a way that facilitates their growth." More thoughtful silence followed, and then a pastor reflected, "I thought when I went into ministry that I would be having deep spiritual conversations with my church members about their relationships with God. But it seems that all I talk to people about are their problems and complaints. And, if I'm honest, I've gotten to the point where I'm more focused on making them happy than on anything else." Another said, "Yeah, it's like we spend so much time talking to people and have had so little guidance about how to do it well." Underlying the words and tone of this discussion, I perceived a desire to help people love themselves, their neighbors, and God more fully and completely. These ministers were expressing a longing for the ability to facilitate their parishioners' growth toward love.

Think for a moment about your experiences of conversations with the parishioners who ask for your help. Perhaps you identify with one or more of these ministers. Perhaps you recognize the longing to help people grow toward love. You may be facing some of the problems described earlier in this chapter, or you may have additional concerns. You might be a beginner wanting to learn the basics in order to prevent these troubles. Consider your own situation and the questions, difficulties, or concerns that you currently face. What would you like to improve?

Solutions This Book Offers

Once you are clear about where you are, the next step is to think about where you want to be regarding your ministry conversations. As you imagine where you want to be when you have completed this book, what particular problems do you hope to solve? What goals do you long to reach? I imagine that, whatever your specific situation, you yearn to be a spiritual and powerful guide when congregants ask for your assistance. Like the ministers described above, you hope to facilitate your parishioners' growth toward love.

Help is available! This book will teach you a process for ministry conversations that provides a solution for many of the problems that plague ministers. For example, it would be a great relief to have a reliable methodology to follow rather than floundering and struggling through conversations. The procedure specified in *CARING: Six Steps for Effective Pastoral Conversations* offers you both a dependable process to follow and expectations that are more realistic for yourself and your congregants. You will then be able to clearly communicate realistic expectations to the persons who ask for your help and to guide them through a process to effectively address their concerns.

The CARING process for pastoral conversations can be used in brief discussions, as well as in longer, scheduled pastoral dialogues, thus allowing you to adjust to the time you have available. It will help you guide parishioners through a systematic process, thus making effective use of the time you do have available. To be a good steward of your time, you might choose to limit the number of helping sessions you offer to any one person. Following the CARING model is an effective way to provide assistance in one conversation or in a limited number of meetings.

You will learn specific techniques to help your congregants master their fears, overcome their doubts, and get around their obstacles. Having the skills to assist congregants with these distressing difficulties will bring more ease and effectiveness to your work. You will become crystal clear about which responsibilities belong to you and which ones belong to the person you are helping. These solutions will lower your stress and increase your satisfaction in your pastoral conversations.

As you consider where you want to be regarding your ministry conversations, the subtitle of this book might have captured your imagination. You earnestly desire the ability to create effective pastoral conversations. You long to know how to lead your congregants through a powerful problem-solving process that also fosters spiritual growth. You want a reliable, step-by-step process that you can depend upon to work consistently. The method offered in *CARING: Six Steps for Effective Pastoral Conversations* facilitates people's ability to solve their problems and reach for their goals. As you help your parishioners with their concerns, you will also help them grow spiritually. You will have knowledge and skills to guide them toward meaningful personal, emotional, and spiritual growth. You will make a deep and powerful difference in your congregants' lives. Mastering the six steps to effective pastoral conversations will make your ministry more competent, easier, and more joyful.

CARING offers a trustworthy method for listening well, understanding your parishioners' concerns, and guiding them to discern the next steps in solving their problems or moving toward their goals. I understand spiritual growth as learning to have more loving relationships with all aspects of yourself, other people, and God. Your congregants are seeking spiritual care whenever they ask for help to improve their own lives, their relationships, or their connections with God. You hold in your hands a powerful conversational process in which growth toward love occurs within the context of the ordinary (and extraordinary) struggles, concerns, and pains of life. Applying the six steps to your ministry transforms your helping conversations, as you competently and reliably facilitate both problem-solving and spiritual growth.

Coaching as a Resource for Ministers

I have been a minister and pastoral care professional for three decades, working as a minister with children and youth; a chaplain; a pastoral counselor; a spiritual guide; and an ACPE certified educator (formerly called CPE Supervisor). The methodology I have developed for ministers to conduct effective pastoral conversations integrates the disciplines of ministry, particularly pastoral care and spiritual guidance, with the newer field of coaching. While you will be familiar with areas of ministry, you may need to be introduced to life coaching as one of the resources I use in the six steps of highly effective pastoral conversations. I have been testing and refining these steps since I experienced my first training as a life coach in 2006 with the On Purpose Group, and particularly since I completed life coach training through the Martha Beck Institute in 2017.

Two ordinary uses for the word coach can serve as metaphors to help you understand the process of life coaching. Perhaps the word coach is most commonly used in athletics. The coach helps the athlete develop skills and strategies to compete in his or her sport. The coach provides assistance, resources, techniques, and support. The athlete prepares, practices, and plays the game. The athlete reaps the benefits and drawbacks of action and inaction. As a minister, you can coach people to develop skills and action plans for living and growing spiritually. Your parishioners are responsible for their choices, their actions and inactions, and their results.

In England, the word coach means a vehicle of transportation, like a bus. A stagecoach in the American West was a vehicle of transportation that persons used to travel to new frontiers. Coaching is a process that helps people move from where they are to where they want to be. Ministers can draw from the skills of coaching to effectively help individuals travel to new frontiers in their lives.

The International Coach Federation (ICF) is an organization that was formed to advance coaching as a profession. On its website, the ICF defines coaching as "partnering with clients in a thought-provoking and creative process that inspires them to maximize their personal and professional potential."[1] While you are more likely to be called upon to help your parishioners with their personal growth, at times you might be asked to help with questions related to professional issues. Inspiring people to maximize their potential is a goal that ministers share with coaches.

Martha Beck, Inc. (MBI) offers life coach training based on Beck's theories and practices. Drawing from her education at Harvard as a PhD-level sociologist, Beck has developed tools coaches use to help people grow and change. The "About Martha" section of her website accurately reports that Beck regularly updates her methodologies based on ongoing research in a variety of disciplines including psychology and neuroscience.[2] In the introduction to her book *Steering by Starlight: Find Your Right Life, No Matter What!* Beck describes her work as "understanding how to build a life worth living."[3] Beck elaborates that she had developed tools to help herself find her best life and then she began teaching them to others.[4] Helping people experience life at its best is also a goal that ministers share with coaches. Beck's tools, along with other material from the field of life coaching, are beneficial resources for ministers.

An Integrated Process
(Pastoral Care, Spiritual Direction, and Coaching)

The CARING methodology makes use of the unique gifts I have discovered in pastoral care, spiritual direction, and life coaching. Benefits I have received from pastoral care include self-awareness, self-management, relationship skills, and depth of understanding and reflection. Spiritual direction offers attention to the work of God in the midst of all of life, as well as practices for listening to God, according to the teacher of spiritual direction Tilden Edwards.[5] Life coaching offers an attention to focus, goals, and strategizing,[6] as well as releasing or working around obstacles, according to Coach U, Inc.[7] Each field provides significant strengths and contributions to my CARING methodology for pastoral conversations.

The integration of resources from life coaching, pastoral care, and spiritual direction makes the procedure for guiding pastoral conversations offered in this book distinctive. The six steps provide a new process for ministry conversations in which the particular strengths of each field are harnessed. The areas of emphasis and potencies of each discipline contribute to the CARING pastoral conversation. For example, life coaching's emphasis on focus, strategy, and action adds to the emphasis on deep understanding and reflection often found in pastoral care and spiritual direction. On the other hand, attention to personal and spiritual growth keeps the goal orientation of coaching from becoming distorted or out of alignment with a person's spirituality. The emphasis on understanding where God is in the midst of the situation provides powerful spiritual resources not always utilized in life coaching. The six steps of effective pastoral conversations are a uniquely balanced process that I developed, through much trial and error, as I worked to integrate these disciplines.

Overview of the Six Steps (CARING)

Most parishioners value a minister's ability to guide them toward their goals and dreams or to solve their problems. CARING teaches a basic introductory framework for pastoral conversations that helps persons achieve their goals or solve their problems. The methodology taught in this book is not intended for counseling, crisis intervention, or the ministry of presence. Other resources are available to teach you these important types of pastoral care. The methodology provided in this book is a spiritual process to powerfully guide parishioners who seek help solving their problems or reaching their goals.

Here is an overview of the ministry process designed to help you have powerful, effective, and spiritual conversations that help your congregants find solutions to their problems and move toward their dreams. I use the acronym CARING to facilitate remembering the steps of the process. Note that each step is something that you invite the person to do in partnership with you. Here are the six steps to follow in pastoral conversations:

C—Connect with God, self, and others

A—Attend to the journey and assess the need

R—Reach clarity about the realistic focus for this conversation

I—Inspire the development of a loving action plan

N—Navigate around obstacles to the plan

G—Generate commitment to a specific, loving action plan

The CARING model can be utilized in any conversation when your parishioners ask for your help to reach a goal or solve a problem, unless you discern that you need to provide crisis ministry or refer the person for specialized help. The steps can be used when people ask for your help in informal settings, as well as when you have a scheduled appointment with a congregant.

Overview of the Book

The six steps are discussed in the next six chapters. I am providing a brief summary of each chapter here. Seeing the overview of the whole process will make it easier for you to understand how each step fits into the whole and how the entire process works. Consider these summaries to be appetizers before the main course.

Chapter 1 offers guidelines for beginning a ministry conversation, including both long-term and short-term preparation. Then it focuses on the first step: Connect with God, Self, and Others. Each of these types of connection is described so that pastoral conversations can begin effectively. Practices and techniques are provided to help persons connect with God and with their own inner wisdom. Guidelines are offered so that you can facilitate an effective helping relationship. The work of connection is foundational, and it prepares you and your parishioner for the second step.

Chapter 2 focuses on the second step: Attend to the Journey and Assess the Need. Attending to the journey includes exploring where the person is, what difficulties are being experienced, and where the person wants to be. Guidelines are provided for how to address these three aspects of the journey. After hearing the person's story, you must assess what kind of help the individual needs and choose how to proceed, such as continuing the conversation, conducting another type of ministry conversation such as education or crisis intervention, or making a referral. Guidelines are provided for making the assessment; resources are offered for other types of ministry conversations and referrals; and suggestions are given for continuing with a pastoral conversation.

After understanding the person's situation, you are ready to provide specific help. Chapter 3 focuses on step three of the CARING process: Reach Clarity about the Realistic Focus for This Conversation. This chapter describes the characteristics of effective goals and teaches you how to facilitate arriving at a realistic and helpful focus for the conversation. Doing this step well makes the rest of the conversation easier, more focused, and more effective.

The fourth step follows naturally from step three because, as people become clear about a goal, they automatically begin to look for ways to meet it. Chapter 4 addresses step four: Inspire the Development of a Loving Action Plan. Creating an inspired action plan to reach the goal of the conversation will include inviting help from God, the person's higher self, and other people. The section about help from God includes a discussion of being sensitive to the individual's theology and spirituality, as well as offering practices to facilitate listening to God. The discussion of help from the person's higher self includes a variety of questions to help people discover their own inner wisdom. The section about help from other people includes a discussion of how to brainstorm with your congregant, as well as ways to invite the person to access memories and awareness of other people who can provide assistance.

As this discussion of possible actions is taking place, obstacles may become apparent, or you may need to ask your congregant about blocks or resistance. Addressing these obstacles is the goal of chapter 5, which discusses step five: Navigate around Obstacles to the Plan. This chapter provides guidelines, techniques, and practices for leading people to overcome their obstacles. Many times untrue and fearful thoughts, feelings, and belief systems sabotage growth. This chapter gives you tools to assist your congregants in changing these self-sabotaging behaviors by choosing truth over falsehood and loving actions in response to fear.

The sixth step builds upon all the previous steps. Chapter 6 teaches you how to facilitate step six: Generate Commitment to a Specific, Loving Action Plan. You are given guidelines to help people choose specific, loving actions. This chapter also discusses the importance of specifying when, where, and how actions will be taken. Support and accountability are addressed. Finally, recommendations are provided for ending the pastoral conversation.

The conclusion summarizes the contributions of this book and offers further applications to ministry. It details how problems have been transformed into solutions. Suggestions are given for the next steps of your journey. The book concludes with encouragement and support, as well as recognition of your growth in grace, community, integrity, and love.

Learning the CARING process will give you clear steps to follow in order to confidently help your parishioners. You will have skills and tools to guide people to access wisdom that can assist them in solving their problems. These steps will function like gutter guards in a bowling alley that keep the ball in the lane. They will be boundaries to help you function safely and competently within your role as minister. You will do less floundering and following tangents, and will ask more powerful and purposeful questions. You will guide your congregants to discover action plans that will improve their lives and help them grow toward love.

Imagine the freedom you will feel when you know that your job is not to fix the problem or find the answer. Your job is to follow a reliable process, ask powerful questions, and facilitate people's connection to their own spirituality and resources. Finding the answers is your parishioners' job! CARING will teach you how to guide persons to find their own wise and loving answers by receiving help from God, their own inner wisdom, and other people. The six steps will invite spirituality and creativity into pastoral conversations. Your ministry will become easier, more powerful, and more loving.

How to Use This Book

Remember your vision of where you would like to be when you have finished this book. Which solutions do you hope to make your own? You may want to solve some of the problems I have mentioned, or there may be other issues you would like to address. What are the goals you would like to accomplish as you learn to conduct more effective pastoral conversations that address people's concerns, include spiritual resources, and lead to spiritual growth?

I suggest that you write down the specific questions that you hope this book will help you answer and the skills that you would like to develop or improve. Writing your concerns down will help you read with more focus upon discovering solutions. At the end of this book I will invite you to review your questions and consolidate your learning. You can write your hopes down at the end of this chapter, at the end of this book, or in a notebook that you keep as you read.

Read and practice the concepts and skills in each chapter with your own goals in mind. It is appropriate to practice these concepts with your own problems as you deepen your understanding of each step. You might also find a practice partner, perhaps another minister, to help you learn this process and make it your own. With permission, you might practice with family members and friends. I remember working with my son, who was about eight years old when I first trained as a life coach. He asked me one day, "Mom, can we do that thing where we talk, and then I tell you what I'm going to do?"

As you practice, a few distinctions are important for you to remember. Beginning with smaller problems that do not have a big emotional charge is always a good idea. Also, remember that this process is about helping people find their own answers, not giving them your solutions. If you are practicing with family and friends, be careful that you are not invested in giving them advice. You will need to discern if you can practice guiding them to find solutions without offering advice as a friend or family member. Another distinction that is important to remember is that this process is not about counseling or intervening in crisis. Be certain that the topics you address are appropriate for a ministry conversation about solving problems or reaching goals.

If you are using this book in a seminary classroom or a clinical pastoral education program, make use of the available feedback and education. Good teaching and supervision will vastly improve your skills. If you are working on your own, consider seeking a supervisor, consultant, or a practice partner.

Finally, know that reading without taking action on your new knowledge will have limited effectiveness. Learning a new skill, like learning to ride a bike, calls for trying, falling down, determining what you did wrong, trying again, and improving as you go, until you have mastered the skill. Create and take advantage of opportunities to practice this methodology.

I am excited about the possibilities that lie before you as you learn to have CARING conversations. My own ministry of pastoral conversations took a quantum leap when I developed this process. The combination of using spiritual reflection and resources, making careful choices about focus and goals, seeking inspiration from God, accessing inner wisdom, receiving help from other people, navigating around obstacles, and developing a clear and loving action plan was amazingly powerful. I experienced less worry and anxiety, and more confidence and peace. As I taught this process to ministers, I found that they, too, experienced more confidence, effectiveness, and peace. Transformation awaits you! I hope that you will find renewed joy, purpose, and love in your ministry conversations. Let us begin.

Chapter One

STEP 1: CONNECT WITH GOD, SELF, AND OTHERS

The focus of this chapter is the first step, which is to connect with God, self, and others. These connections will help you to be prepared for your ministry conversations and to begin these conversations well. Focusing on being connected with God, yourself, and other people is a way of life that gives you long-term, ongoing preparation for ministry conversations. Preparing yourself for helping conversations can also happen in the hours or days before the ministry encounter. Finally, as pastoral conversations begin, you will guide people to connect with God, their own inner wisdom, and other people, including you.

Your Long-Term Preparation

If your way of living includes connecting with God intentionally, then you will be more prepared for your own connection with God to be a deliberate part of your helping conversations. You will also be more prepared to guide your congregants to connect with God at the beginning of a conversation in which they seek your guidance. I hope that you practice spiritual disciplines that help you connect with God on a regular basis. These disciplines could include prayer, meditation, journaling, and many others. If you have allowed these practices to fall away, I encourage you to renew your own practices to communicate with God and to experiment with new ways of connecting with God.

Connecting with your own inner world intentionally throughout your life will also prepare you to do so during ministry conversations as you guide your parishioners to connect to their own inner wisdom. Developing greater self-awareness is a long-term, ongoing process that will help you to be prepared for pastoral conversations. Methods for connecting with yourself should be practices that you do regularly. Journaling, mindfulness, and noticing your feelings and thoughts are techniques that will help you bring more self-awareness to your pastoral conversations. Another fruitful avenue is working with a coach, spiritual director, ACPE pastoral educator, or therapist. Understanding and connecting with the deeper and wiser part of yourself provide significant groundwork for supporting your parishioners in solving their problems or reaching their goals.

Developing strong relationship skills will also prepare you for ministry conversations. Awareness of other people, empathy, and compassion will improve your ministry. Listening well is a skill to be developed over time that will enhance your pastoral conversations. Empathic listening will be discussed in chapter 2. Clinical pastoral education, therapy, and spiritual direction are all resources that can help you grow in this area.

You are providing long-term preparation for your parishioners whenever you teach them how to connect with God, such as through sermons, Bible studies, retreats, and individual or group spiritual guidance sessions. You can focus on topics like how to pray, how to use scripture as a tool to connect with God, how to journal with the goal of connecting with God, and how to heal any difficulties in connecting with God. Look for resources from the literature of spiritual formation, spiritual disciplines, Christian spirituality, and specific disciplines like prayer, meditation, and journaling.

Along with preparing people ahead of time spiritually, you will also want to communicate practical matters about your policies of providing care. You will be better able to connect to yourself and the person with whom you are ministering if you have clear policies in place for how you provide help for your congregants. How many sessions you offer, how you work with people, what level and understanding of confidentiality you use, and how you deal with the need for a referral are all matters that you will want to clarify for yourself and your congregants.[1] You can communicate your policies to your congregants ahead of time in a variety of ways. Hospital and institutional pastoral care departments will have written policies provided to patients and residents in accordance with the procedures of the institution. Churches could make pastoral care policies available in church covenants, on websites, or in written documents available to people before their first appointments.

Your Short-Term Preparation: Before the Conversation

When the person asks you to help him with a problem, you might hear indications that his concern does not fall within the parameters of a CARING pastoral conversation. If it is clear that the situation is a crisis, you will want to provide crisis ministry immediately.[2] If it is clear that the person is looking for help that does not involve problem-solving, such as information or education, you can provide it in this initial conversation or make an appointment to address the question later. If you are unsure what your parishioner is requesting and the situation is not a crisis, you can schedule an appointment to meet with him. As you then follow the CARING process, the first two steps will help you determine the best type of conversation for helping the person.

Just after the congregant has asked for an appointment is a good time to communicate the essentials of your policies about providing spiritual care to people. Depending on the circumstances and the language that your parishioner understands, you might want to clarify that you provide "pastoral care" or "spiritual care" or "ministry." You should be clear that you do not provide mental health care or psychotherapy or counseling, but that you can refer him to professionals for these services if needed.[3] It is also important to communicate the limits to confidentiality in your ministry conversations, taking into account the laws of your state. For example, your own ethical convictions and/or the laws in your state might necessitate your reporting plans for suicide or homicide, or evidence of elder or child abuse to agencies that will work to keep people safe. Reviewing the literature of ministry and determining these policies for your setting is part of your overall preparation for helpful conversations.

It is also a good idea to clarify how many sessions you provide for your congregants. I recommend setting a limit to the number of sessions to allow for good stewardship of your time and your responsibility to the entire congregation. Following the guidance of pastoral care texts, you will want to decide your own policies about the number of sessions you will offer. Some topics can be addressed in a session or two. I believe that three or four sessions is a good limit for most ministers. Some experts consider six sessions as the most that a minister should offer about any particular topic.[4] If a person needs more assistance than can be offered in a limited number of sessions, then a referral for specialized or longer-term help is in order.

The CARING process taught in this book is designed to be completed in one conversation. Many times this methodology guides your parishioner to make an action plan in one session that will be sufficient help for her. At other times, you might have more than one conversation about the same topic, and each conversation should follow all six steps of the process. As you grow more experienced with the process, you may find yourself modifying it for your own work, perhaps conducting the first half of the conversation in one session and the second half in a later session.

When a congregant schedules an appointment, the person is indicating readiness to receive your help. The issue is possibly a problem that she has wrestled with for some time. You can help the person by expressing hope and confidence that you can guide her to seek God's help and develop a plan that will address her concerns. You could speak of coaching the person to solve her problem. Another alternative would be to spell out your approach by saying something like, "I will help you explore your situation, listen to God and your own inner wisdom, and come up with a plan of action." Experiment with finding your own way to describe how you help people to solve their problems.

When a conversation has been scheduled, you have time to pay attention to your connections with God, yourself, and your congregant before the meeting. You prepare the way ahead of time for a powerful conversation that will help the person grow to be more loving as he solves his problems. You can experiment with how far in advance to prepare for your ministry conversations. Looking over your calendar a few days to a week ahead in order to pray and prepare for your ministry conversations can be a meaningful practice.

An advantage of doing so is that you have time to address any concerns that you notice about ministry with this person at this time. You might feel uneasy or reluctant to help a particular person who is on your calendar. While you may be tempted to believe that these feelings are a failure on your part, there is a better way to understand them. Feelings are a sign that something needs your attention. In fact, Gretchen Rubin, bestselling author about happiness and habits, postulates, "Negative emotions like loneliness, envy, and guilt have an important role to play in a happy life; they're big, flashing signs that something needs to change."[5]

Your feelings of unease or reluctance to help someone might be signaling you that something needs to change. You can ask yourself several questions in order to heed the message of your reluctance. Is there something you need to do to be better prepared? If your conversations with this person tend to go badly, review the issues and make the changes needed. You might choose to consult with a colleague or supervisor to clarify the issues and your best response.

Is your reluctance to see the person coming from any of the issues David Switzer lists as reasons to refer? Some of Switzer's guidelines are straightforward, such as referring persons who show signs of psychosis or depression, or who are addicted to drugs or alcohol. Additional guidelines for referral are more subtle but also important, such as you don't understand what is happening, you are anxious when you are with the person, or you want to stop others from helping the person.[6] Switzer's guidelines for when to refer are well worth reviewing and committing to memory.

If the situation calls for referral, you can draw from several resources in pastoral care. Switzer offers guidelines about how and where to refer. He outlines the importance of time, sensitivity, and skill in making a referral so that people do not feel rejected. He describes both the process of communicating about referral and the specifics of referring to people, agencies, institutions, or programs.[7] Margaret Kornfeld, in *Cultivating Wholeness,* devotes an entire chapter to preparing for referral.[8] She concludes the chapter with guidelines for referral that include introducing the idea early in the pastoral conversation, gathering data, organizing the information, and choosing an appropriate resource.[9]

Of course, when you feel uneasy about ministry with a particular person, you can also pray about the difficulties that you are sensing. Even if you are unaware of any issues, praying about your upcoming ministry encounters can be powerful preparation for the ministry conversation. You will also benefit from the habit of taking a few minutes before your appointments to prepare by connecting with God, yourself, and with your understanding of your parishioner's needs. Scheduling conversations with a cushion of time before and after for prayer and reflection will make your ministry conversations more deliberate, constructive, and powerful.

Your Connection with God

Just before the conversation begins, you would be wise to pay attention to your own connection with God, yourself, and your parishioner. Breathe deeply to deliberately connect with God. In many spiritual traditions, the breath is an honored way to connect with God. In the Christian tradition, breath carries many symbolic meanings. God breathed the breath of life into human beings at creation.[10] Jesus breathed on his disciples and invited them to "receive the Holy Spirit" (John 20:22). One deep deliberate breath can reconnect you with God at the beginning of a conversation (or anytime, really) especially if you are intentionally seeking to experience God's presence.

If you are anxious about how the conversation will go, a deep breath to connect with God will remind you of the help and support God provides for you. If you are worried or distracted about something else, breathing deeply to connect with God can help you bring your focus to this particular parishioner. If you are prone to take on other people's feelings or anxieties, a deliberate connection with God through your breath can help stabilize you.

Prayer is an obvious way to connect with God prior to a ministry conversation. You might begin with acknowledging your reliance upon God and your desire to be of service to God and the other person. You can ask for help with any particular challenges that you foresee. You can connect with the love of God that undergirds you and your parishioner, which goes before you, and which exists within you.

Your Connection with Self

As you connect with the love of God that is within you, you are also connecting with the deeper and wiser part of yourself. This aspect of yourself is important to notice in your ministry. Theologians and writers about Christian spirituality refer to a higher, wiser, and larger part of ourselves. The ancient term for this aspect of ourselves is the soul. For example, St. Teresa of Avila says, "Because we have heard and because faith tells us so, we know we have souls. But we seldom consider the precious things that can be found in this soul, or who dwells within it, or its high value."[11] Richard Rohr uses the term "true self" for the soul that he labeled "God-in-you."[12] Rohr describes the soul as "vast, silent, restful, and resourceful,"[13] and he reflects, "Your soul is much larger than you! You are just along for the ride. When you learn to live there, you live with everyone and everything else too. . . . Inside your True Self, you know you are not alone, and you foundationally 'belong' to God and to the universe (1 Corinthians 3:23)."[14] Psychotherapist and author about the spiritual aspects of human life Christina Grof says, "The deeper Self is benevolent, loving, and wise."[15]

I am not claiming that all of these authors are referring to precisely the same aspect of ourselves. Nor am I suggesting some type of synthesis of these ideas. I do want to illustrate a mysterious truth that my experiences with personal growth, spiritual growth, and ministry have taught me. Human beings do have a higher, wiser, deeper, larger, and true aspect of ourselves that we can learn to access for help and guidance. Accessing your own higher self and guiding your parishioners to do so can significantly improve your ministry conversations.

Before the conversation begins you can set your intention to listen to your higher self. You can also intend to be wise and discerning about which ideas are from your higher self and which are from another part of you, such as unloving and unwise beliefs that you absorbed from other people. A spiritual director once told me that I sometimes confused the voices of my higher self and the Holy Spirit with the voices of my tyrannical conscience that had been formed in part by extended family and culture. He taught me to ask the questions "Is it true?" and "Is it loving?" to help me discern the differences.

As you are connecting with the higher, wiser, more loving part of yourself, you can become aware of any concerns that you have about ministry with this person at this time. If you are tired, if you are worried about something in your own life, if you are distracted by a personal or church issue, set those things aside in order to give your congregant your full attention. As the conversation begins, you can intend to stay connected with yourself throughout the conversation. Some of the best insights about your parishioner's needs will come from paying attention to your own responses to the person as the conversation develops.

Your Connection with Your Parishioner

Before the conversation begins you can take a deep breath and become aware of your pastoral concern for your parishioner. Notice your common humanity and your common faith. Be curious and open to learning something new about this person.

A number of items regarding your connection with your parishioner are important as you are preparing to begin your conversation. Remember that it is your job to guide people to create the changes they desire. It is not your job to change them or to make something happen. This knowledge allows you to let go of the burden of having all the answers, knowing everything, or pretending that you do. Through your relationship with your parishioner, you can help that person access the resources of her higher self. You facilitate the person's connection with her higher self, and she listens for answers and wisdom. As you emotionally connect with your parishioner, you do so as the facilitator of the person's discovering her own wisdom rather than as the one who is expected to bring wisdom to the situation. This change enables you to offer more relaxed and more effective ministry. It releases you from assuming responsibilities that do not belong to you.

Connecting with God, yourself, and your parishioner can be done briefly with a deep breath or two. It takes longer to read the description than to do the action recommended. You may want to develop your own personal, shorthand way of connecting with God, your higher self, and your parishioner before you begin a pastoral conversation. I like to take three or four deep breaths while repeating a phrase with each one. Breath number one—I am connecting with God (on the inhale), and I invite God's help (on the exhale). Breath number two—I am connecting with my higher wisdom (on the inhale), and I invite my higher self to help (on the exhale). Breath number three—I am my parishioner's (call by name) pastor (on the inhale), and I will facilitate his own connection with God (on the exhale). Sometimes I only have time for one breath before beginning the conversation because the person is eager to get started. In those circumstances, this is what I do: I take one deep breath silently asking for God's help. On the inhale, I silently say, "Help me to connect" and on the exhale I silently say, "With You, my higher self, and my parishioner."

I once invited a class of about twenty students to each choose one way of connecting prior to a ministry conversation that would be meaningful to him or her. Each student chose something unique including scriptures, hymns, and short prayers. I invite you now to choose a way of connecting with God, yourself, and your parishioner that you could use to prepare yourself prior to ministry conversations. Experiment with this particular method and see how it works. You might need to try several ways of connecting before you find one that is effective for you.

Begin the Conversation
(Scheduled Meetings)

At the beginning of pastoral conversations, you will guide your parishioners to connect with God, their own higher selves, and other people who can support them. Connecting with you first is most natural. Your parishioner will enter your office. You will say hello, invite the person to sit down, and perhaps begin with brief social conversation. You might ask about the traffic or the weather. You could ask if he had any problems finding your office if he is not familiar with it. You may have other topics you already use routinely, and if you know the person you might have more relevant topics to offer. The emotional connection you make with the person is more important than the details of this social conversation. I avoid the question "How are you today?" because people sometimes hear it as an invitation to begin talking about the problem, and I want to help them connect with me, their own inner wisdom, and God before hearing about their concern.

Your previous relationship with the person and your quick assessment of what he seems to need at the beginning of the conversation will inform your decisions about how to conduct the start of the conversation. If you know the person well and your pastoral relationship is already established, the beginning social conversation can be very brief. He may be ready to get down to business right away. In this case you can move directly to the Connect step of a ministry conversation. If you know him well but he seems a little nervous, a few minutes of relaxed social conversation can help him get prepared to talk with you as he remembers and experiences his connection with you. Then, the Connect step of the CARING process provides more help as the person prepares to discuss the problem.

If your ministry is like mine, sometimes persons will sit down and immediately launch into talking about their problems. Often, by the time people come to see us, they have tried to solve the problem on their own. They are feeling their need for help, and sometimes their desperation comes through as they immediately begin telling you about their problem. I used to follow their lead and move right into the attending step of the conversation. I believed that their connection with me was already established and that they were demonstrating connection with God by choosing to see a minister.

I discovered over time that these conversations did not go as well as those that begin with a structured (even if brief) connecting process. I realized that while people who started by discussing their problem immediately were connected to me as their minister, they might not be consciously connected with God or with their higher selves. I began gently stopping people, saying something such as, "Let me interrupt you for a minute. I do want to hear about this problem. It's important to you, and I want to help you the best way I can. I have learned that taking a minute to connect with God and with our own inner wisdom will make it easier to explore the problem and find solutions."

This intervention shifts the attitude of the conversation. Without an intentional step to Connect with God, her higher self, and other people, the person is speaking to you without being intentionally aware of her resources. With the introduction of the Connect step, you facilitate the other person to recognize relationships and resources that can bring support and help. This guidance invites the person to access her connection with God and her higher wisdom.

In my experience, people receive this kind of leadership with gratitude. They often seem relieved that I am guiding the conversation to begin with an awareness of spiritual resources. Often, the tension in their bodies relaxes. I sometimes sense recognition of the wisdom of what I am suggesting. I have the feeling that the person might be thinking, "Of course, I should have known that. Doing that will help."

Having approached this situation both by skipping the formal Connect step and by intentionally connecting, I have come to believe that deliberately taking time to connect is more effective. In addition to the benefits described above, I have also found that people do a better job Attending to the Journey (step two) when they have first Connected (step one). They generally speak more carefully and explore their concerns with more depth and honesty. In addition, I provide better ministry because taking the Connect step allows me to intentionally connect with God, my higher wisdom, and the other person. I am then more prepared to listen well when we get to the attending stage.

Introduce the Process

An important part of connecting with your parishioner is to introduce the conversation. I find it helpful to share a few basic concepts with my congregants. Naming my assumptions helps people follow and participate more fully in the process as I guide them. I usually say something like, "In this conversation I hope to help you find ways to get from the problem you are currently experiencing to where you want to be. I will guide the conversation so that you can access your own inner wisdom and your relationship with God. I believe that you have more wisdom and inner resources than you know, and I'll be trying to help you discover them. I see it as my job to guide the conversation and ask good questions so that you can find the solutions that will work best for you. I believe you are the expert about your own life. You know far more than I do about the problem we are going to discuss and about your situation." I might not use every sentence with every person exactly like this example, but these are the points that I feel are important for people to understand. I encourage you to experiment with specific phrases and sentences that you would feel comfortable using with your particular parishioners.

With some people that approach seems to be enough and I can then move straight to guiding the conversation through the Connect process. When someone seems to want a little more from me, I add, "I plan to guide you through a six-step process that is designed to explore the problem, seek alternatives and help, and create an action plan to solve the problem. I'll ask focused questions. I'll invite you to explore them and find your own answers. You will leave with a plan of action."

Again, I encourage you to experiment. Find the phrases and sentences that will be appropriate for your context and comfortable for your congregants. Write things down that might work. Consider what theological, biblical, or spiritual concepts would be easy for you to communicate and for your congregants to understand as you explain your approach.

Several intangibles will help you to establish a strong helping relationship with a parishioner who asks for your help. You can use body language that communicates your care and pastoral concern for the individual. Appropriate eye contact, an open posture, a comfortable tone of voice that is both matter of fact and caring are all behaviors that help people feel more connected with us. These qualities are helpful whether this is our first time to talk with a particular person, or we have had numerous ministry conversations over the years.

Guide the Connecting Experience

People often respond to my introduction by saying something like, "That sounds good." I then move directly to helping them Connect. There are several different ways to do this, depending on your context, your style, and your parishioner's personality. If I have talked about the six-step process with someone, I might say, "The first step is to connect with your own inner wisdom, God, and people who might help you." With some people I might ask, "What would help you do that? Pray? Sit in silence for a few minutes? Is there a scripture that we could read or a hymn that we might sing?" In my experience, people most often respond by wanting prayer or silence. If prayer is the answer, I will clarify whether they want to pray aloud or silently. If they want a spoken prayer, I will ask if they want to pray or if they want me to offer the prayer. If they want silence, I usually ask them to say "amen" when they are finished.

Remember that the steps are a mnemonic to help you recall them; they are not words that you have to say to your parishioner. If you want to enter step one more simply, you might choose to say something like, "Why don't we begin by sitting together in silence for a few minutes. This will give you a chance to slow down and get ready to look for answers. You can ask for God's help if you would like. You might connect with your own inner wisdom and resources. You might remember the other people who can support you or be a resource for you." Note that this beginning invites persons to connect with God, their higher selves, and other people.

You might be wondering why I qualified asking for God's help with the words *if you like*. I add this modifier because sometimes when people are troubled, praying may be difficult for them. Be sensitive to the fact that some people may be reluctant to pray at the beginning of the conversation. In addition, some pastoral conversations are with people whose faith background and spiritual commitments the minister does not know. In that case, you can use modifiers as described above. You can use terms such as "the divine" if you believe to do so would be helpful. You might choose to ask people how they understand God, so that your leadership can be most helpful to them by using concepts and language they find meaningful.

If the ministry conversation you are beginning is one of a series of conversations or a follow-up to a previous pastoral conversation, you will want to reconnect with the person briefly. A brief period of social conversation is often helpful. I recommend waiting until step two, Attend to the Journey, before hearing the person's report about his work on the previous plan. I find that the report is more focused and thoughtful if it comes after the connecting phase rather than before it. Also, logically, hearing about the person's successes and struggles with the plan he developed in the last session is a natural part of attending to where he is now.

To recap, begin a scheduled conversation with brief social conversation that is appropriate to the relationship you have with the person. Introduce your process to the person in a way that is appropriate to your relationship and what he already knows. Then lead him through the connecting process. We will turn now to discussing unscheduled conversations.

Begin the Conversation
(Unscheduled Requests for Help)

One aspect of ministry that is disconcerting to new ministers is that wherever we go, we are likely to see someone who recognizes us as persons of God and looks to us for guidance. This experience is as likely to happen at the grocery store as it is at church. Therefore, people may approach us seeking spiritual care at any time and in any place. Successful ministers have learned to deal graciously with this reality, making on the spot decisions about conducting a conversation immediately or scheduling an appointment for a later time. These decisions call for listening to yourself and to God.

Listen to Yourself

Listening to yourself is important in all of ministry. It is particularly crucial as you decide how to respond to impromptu requests for help. Your feelings can be subtle. For example, you might feel a slight uneasiness about being overheard if you are in a social setting. When you consider this possibility, you may realize that you are concerned that the person might not have the kind of privacy needed for this particular discussion, so you move to a different part of the room or schedule the conversation for a later time.

Listen to God

Listening to God is important in all of ministry. Your ministry will be more effective if you can learn to notice "the still small

18

voice" (see 1 Kgs 19:12 KJV and NKJV)[16] when you receive a parishioner's impromptu request for your help. Your own practice of discernment is useful here. It is important to know the difference between guidance from God and the "shoulds" and "oughts" that we all have inherited from parents and authorities. We often hear these messages in our minds as we are making decisions. We easily confuse many other voices with the voice of God. I remember a spiritual director telling me that he did not think the Holy Spirit used the concept "should." When you receive an impromptu request, listen with discernment for God's leadership about your response. If you are uncertain, the guidelines that follow can provide some assistance.

Make the Decision

The next step is to decide whether to conduct the conversation here and now or to schedule it for another time and place. If the situation is a crisis, you will not use the CARING process of pastoral conversations because CARING was not designed for crisis ministry. Instead you will follow the procedures of crisis ministry as referenced earlier in this chapter. If the situation is not a crisis, then you will need to decide if it would be appropriate to have a CARING conversation on the spot, or if scheduling an appointment would be better. Some factors to consider are your relationship with the person, the setting, the amount of time that is needed compared with the time you have available, your own energy level, and your other commitments. These judgment calls are sometimes difficult, but if you are mindful of these issues, your decisions will improve.

Establish the Agreement

The minister will then create an agreement for the conversation. You will make it clear to the parishioner whether you will have a pastoral conversation immediately, or if you will schedule a conversation for a later time and a different place. If you have decided that you are available for a conversation immediately, you will also need to consider if the setting is appropriate. It is your job to ensure confidentiality and appropriateness, rather than relying upon the parishioner's judgment. Sometimes people who are in pain will not be as careful about their privacy as they would under normal circumstances. As the professional in the conversation, you must attend to these issues.

If the time and place are appropriate, you can simply say something like, "Would you like to discuss this concern now?" If either the timing or the setting is not appropriate for a pastoral conversation, you will want to suggest an office conversation. Schedule the appointment, or give the person instructions about how to set up an appointment with you.

Appropriately Maintain the Agreement

The minister would then maintain the agreement with the parishioner, conducting a social or pastoral conversation, depending on the agreement. If a later time and place have been agreed upon but the parishioner continues to try to have a pastoral conversation, he may be expressing anxiety about the concern. It may be more pressing than the minister recognized at first. If so, it is appropriate to revisit or renegotiate the plans for the pastoral conversation. If this is not possible, you might need to reassure the person of your willingness to help when the time and place are conducive to discuss the problem. After doing so, you might need to redirect the conversation to something appropriate for the setting.

It takes much more time to describe this process than it does to actually go through it. These procedures are worth perfecting, as ministers must make this type of decision regularly. It is much better to make choices consciously and deliberately with clear reasons than to make decisions without clarity or intentionality.

In unplanned conversations, the person is connecting with you by making a request for help. You might invite a connection with God by saying something as simple as "I trust that God can help us sort this out" or "I pray for God's guidance as we sort this out." You can invite the person to connect with his higher self and other people by saying something like, "As we are exploring this issue, we will seek to discover your own higher wisdom and resources other people might have to offer you" or "You are the expert on your situation; I believe you have solutions to discover." You could also simply ask, "Would you like to have an open-eyed prayer before we explore the problem further?" You might say, "God is with us as we seek a solution for this problem. I also believe that you know more than you think you do, and I can help you discover your own wisdom and answers. I can also help you recognize other people who might support you." In an unplanned conversation, connecting is briefer because the person has already asked you for help.

Pitfalls to Avoid

Whether your conversation is planned or unplanned, there are three pitfalls to avoid during the connection phase. One pitfall is believing that you are the expert who must provide all of the answers. This is too much responsibility for you to assume, as this misunderstanding hampers your connections with yourself, God, and your parishioner. It is not your job to fix the person's problem. It is your job to guide the conversation and to ask good questions. It is your congregant's job to find the answers within and through his relationships with God and other people.

A second pitfall to avoid is an image of God that gets in the way of your ability to connect with God or to guide your congregant to connect with God. If there are distortions in your image of God that cause you to doubt God's love and care, then you are in need of some spiritual growth or healing. A view of God as punishing or judgmental can get in the way of your ability to connect with God and to help others seek God's help and support. If this pitfall occurs for you, please seek resources to heal and improve your image of God. Ask for God's help, and include this issue in your plans for personal spiritual growth.

A third pitfall to avoid is a misuse of the time for this step. Rushing through it keeps you and your congregant from accessing the power and wisdom of your inner worlds and your connections with God. On the other hand, taking too long means that you might shortchange a later aspect of the CARING process. While the steps do not need to be the same length of time in a legalistic way, about one-sixth of the time allotted for the conversation is a reasonable guideline for this stage. So, for a thirty-minute conversation, this step might take about five minutes. As we have already discussed, in some circumstances this step will take less time. Five minutes might also be adequate for an hour-long conversation, leaving more time for later steps.

How to Know You Have Completed This Step

When you have completed the following activities, you have finished this step and are ready to move to the next one.

- You have prepared yourself beforehand by connecting with yourself.

- You have prepared yourself beforehand by connecting with God.

- You have prepared yourself beforehand by reviewing your relationship with the parishioner.

- You have had a social conversation, if needed.

- You have introduced the conversation and described the process for your parishioner.

- You have guided your parishioner to connect with God.

- You have paid attention to your parishioner's connection with you and made any adjustments necessary.

- You have reminded your parishioner of relationships with other people who can offer support (if appropriate).

- You have guided your parishioner's connection with his or her own inner wisdom.

As you move to the next step and throughout the conversation, it will be important for you to stay connected with God, your own higher self, and your parishioner. If you notice that you have lost any of these three connections, you will want to deliberately reconnect, repairing any missteps you might make. Connection is the foundation for all of the other steps, and, done well, will lead you naturally to step two: Attend to the Journey and Assess the Need, which is the subject of the next chapter.

Chapter Two

STEP 2: ATTEND TO THE JOURNEY AND ASSESS THE NEED

Step two of the CARING conversation is Attend to the Journey and Assess the Need. More specifically, step two is attending to the journey from where the person is to where she wants to be, including the difficulties faced. As you attend to the person's journey you will also be assessing what kind of conversation is needed to address the person's concern and, particularly, whether the CARING process is appropriate or whether another type of help is needed.

Because you have connected with the other person, God, and your own wise and loving self, you are now prepared to attend to the person's journey. Your congregant is prepared to share his journey with you because he has connected with you, with his own wise and loving self, and with God. As you attend to your congregant's journey and assess what kind of helping conversation is needed, remember to maintain your connection with God, your higher self, and your parishioner.

Listen Well

Attending to the person's journey and assessing the need begins with listening well. Hearing your parishioner involves seeking to understand the concern of the person, expressing accurate empathy, and responding in ways that let the other know that you are listening. Listening well is difficult. If you doubt the previous assertion, I encourage you to try an exercise I use in my classes. (As is true with all exercises I suggest in this book, be upfront with the person that you are practicing a ministry skill.) Test your listening skills with your learning assistant. For a ten-minute period, allow her to share with you a concern in her life while you listen well.

Your only responses to the person will be to indicate that you are listening. For example, you might make attentive sounds, like "um-hmm" or short phrases like "I see" or "oh my." Your assignment is to listen without interjecting your own opinions or advice. You are not to attempt to solve his problem or to lead him to find a solution. Do not follow any process of guiding a conversation that you learned in your training or use in ministry or social conversations.

The only question you are allowed to ask is one to clarify what the person is saying. Do not ask something such as, "Have you considered doing this…?" That phrase is advice disguised as a question. Your job is simply to hear and comprehend the messages of the other. Seek only to advance your understanding of the person's concerns and to let her know that you are listening to her.

How did it go? If you are like my students, you experienced one of several outcomes. Perhaps you learned that listening is harder work than you realized, and you are not as good at it as you thought. You may also have recognized the importance of listening well to people. The other person told you more than you expected in a short time because of your careful listening. You realized how much can happen in a brief conversation. Your careful listening may have been the catalyst for the person's discovering a solution for his own problem. Students are amazed by how often this happens when they are "only" listening.

An experience of many of my students deserves further elaboration. Often, a student will listen carefully to the concern being expressed. The student does not offer the advice that he would like because of the parameters of the exercise. Then after a few more minutes of listening, it becomes clear to the student that the answer he would have offered will not work given what he now knows of the person's situation. Listening well can prevent much wasted time and advice-giving that is irrelevant because the minister does not fully understand the situation.

If you attend to the person's journey well, the rest of the conversation will flow more easily and effectively. Stephen Covey has an excellent discussion of empathic listening in his *Seven Habits of Highly Effective People*. Covey postulates that there are four levels of listening that we normally use: (1) ignoring the other person; (2) pretending to listen; (3) selective listening, which is hearing only parts of the conversation; and (4) attentive listening, which gives attention and energy to the words being said. He also suggests that there is a very rare fifth level that is the highest type of listening, which he calls empathic listening.[1] He critiques active or reflective listening and contrasts it with empathic listening as follows:

> You listen with reflective skills, but you listen with intent to reply, to control, to manipulate. When I say empathic listening, I mean listening with intent to understand. I mean seeking first to understand, to really understand. It's an entirely different paradigm.[2]

Covey even suggests that empathic listening helps you hear the soul of the other person. As he says:

> Empathic listening is so powerful because it gives you accurate data to work with. Instead of projecting your own autobiography and assuming thoughts, feelings, motives and interpretation, you're dealing with the reality inside another person's head and heart. You're listening to understand. You're focused on receiving the deep communication of another human soul.[3]

At this stage of the CARING process you are seeking to understand the deep, soulful concerns of the other person without offering help or suggestions. Your focus should be on deeply understanding the other, knowing that steps to provide help will come later. The more accurately you understand the person's journey at step two, the more helpful your guidance during later steps will be.

In my experience, seeking to understand the concern of the person through empathic listening requires several types of inner work on the minister's part. First, you must put aside any desire to impress the person with your wisdom, helpfulness, or competence. You will also put aside your wish to be Superman or Wonder Woman, messiah, savior, or rescuer. Second, bring your full attention to the person and her needs, bracketing out anything that stands in the way of being fully present and aware of the person. Third, keep your attention on understanding the individual's concern, holding any solutions that come to mind for later in the conversation if they prove to be appropriate responses.

When your attention wanders to unrelated areas, gently bring it back to the needs of the other. This process is similar to meditation in that when your attention wanders you bring it back to being still in the presence of God. Bringing your attention back to the person reminds you of the value of the person to God and the spiritual significance of all our concerns. This practice is a way to maintain your connection to your parishioner.

Your goal is to fully understand the person's journey. You accomplish this task by attending empathically to the journey. You pay attention to the person, the story, the journey being described. You listen well. You seek to understand the person's experiences. You listen for descriptions of where your congregant is currently and where this person hopes to be in the future. You pay attention to the problem(s) the person hopes to solve and to the concerns expressed. You listen for discussions of what the person has already tried and issues that are blocking the journey. You attend to the journey from where the person is, through the difficulties, to where the person wants to be.

Respond (Let the Other Know You Are Listening)

You will want to offer responses that let your congregant know that you are hearing him. Expressing empathy is a significant way to communicate your care and concern as you listen well. Often, expressing empathy takes the form of short sentences summarizing what you have heard the person say. "It seems that you're feeling sad about that experience" is an example. "You didn't have the motivation to complete the assignment" is another example. Even short exclamations such as "Wow!" or "Oh dear" or "Yikes!" will communicate your concern.

At other times, longer expressions of your empathy are called for. You might summarize what the person has said and recognize the feelings that go along with it. Often, people will respond,

"Yes, that's right. And…" They feel free to tell you more because you understood them. Your responding to them accurately may invite them to explore their concern more completely. At other times people will say, "No, here's what I meant…" Because you were sincerely seeking to understand them, they wish to help you understand their concern. It may also be that they did not express themselves clearly or completely in their initial communication and when you tell them what you heard, it enables them to be clearer and more precise in their own thinking.

All expressions of empathy need to be made with humility, recognizing that your interpretation belongs to you and may or may not be accurate. Your conversation can demonstrate openness to being corrected if you have missed their meanings. You might ask a question such as, "What have I missed or misunderstood?" In my experience, this openness to correction helps people trust you more fully.

Begin the Attending Step

You can make the transition from the connecting step to the attending step in several different ways, depending on what is comfortable for you and appropriate for your parishioner. You might offer clear direction, saying something such as, "The next step of the process we are following is for you to tell me about where you are, where you want to be, and what problems you have experienced as you have tried to get to where you want to be." Some parishioners would appreciate knowing what to expect and having the big picture. Others are ready to talk about their problem and are not looking for particular guidance. With these folks, you might begin more casually, asking something like, "What brought you here today?" or "What is going on?" or "What did you come to see me about?" or "How can I help you?"

Attending to the journey includes listening for three aspects of the person's experience: (1) where the person is currently; (2) what difficulties the person is encountering; and (3) where the person wants to be in the future. As you listen well, seeking understanding of your parishioner's journey, pay attention to which aspects of the journey are being discussed and which ones are being left out. Ask questions to invite her to explore with you all three topics. The order does not matter as long as you cover the current problem, the hopes for the future, and the difficulties being experienced.

You can help your parishioner explore each of these three areas by asking judicious, powerful questions to be certain that you understand where she is, the problems, and where she wants to be. Questions to help you understand where she is include John Patton's three "magic questions." Patton suggests asking "What are you looking for? Why now? Why me?"[4] To ask people what they are looking for can invite them to tell you where they are and where they want to be. You can make this question even more specific and focused by asking "What do you want to get out of this conversation?" or "What do you want to leave with when we are finished with this conversation?" Asking "Why now?" often garners useful information. This question invites your parishioners to share with you anything that precipitated their coming to you for help. "Why me?" is not a request for flattery. The question "Why me?" invites parishioners to verbalize their connection with you that is the reason for choosing to speak to you. It also invites people to reflect on the fact that they have chosen to speak to a minister about their concerns. You can follow up the "Why me?" question with "What made you choose to bring this problem to a minister?" All of these questions can help you attend to the person's journey.

In seeking to understand where the person is, you might hear either circumstances, thoughts, feelings, actions, results, or some or all of these. Drawing from a variety of psychological theories and coaching methodologies, life coach and author Brooke Castillo teaches that circumstances lead to thoughts, which lead to feelings, which influence the person's actions (or lack of action), which lead to the results, which then support or reinforce the person's thoughts.[5]

An example will make this pattern clearer to you. Let us suppose that the circumstance is that a woman is writing a book (ahem). If she thinks this: "I will never get this book finished," then she is likely to feel discouraged or hopeless. These feelings can lead to procrastination or avoidance, which creates the result that the writing is not done. In turn, this lack of writing supports her thought that she will never finish her book.

On the other hand, if she thinks this: "I can finish this book one small step at a time," then she is likely to feel empowered and hopeful. These feelings lead to the actions of making time and having energy to write, with the result that she makes progress on writing her book. This result reinforces her thought "I can finish this book."

Listening for these cycles will help you attend to the person's journey more fully. You will discover that people's experiences often follow this progression. You will want to pay attention to thoughts, feelings, actions, and results, as this concept will be used in later aspects of the CARING process. As the person is describing where he is, it can be useful to listen for and perhaps make written notes of the circumstances, thoughts, feelings, actions, and results. You might ask about any of these topics that the person leaves out of the discussion. You do not need to explore these issues in depth, just notice the circumstances, thoughts, feelings, actions, and results. In a fifty-minute conversation, you will spend perhaps ten minutes on step two, so stay focused on attending to the journey and avoid the temptation to linger here.

Other powerful questions can help you understand where the person wants to be. Obviously, you can simply ask, "Where do you want to be?" or "When this problem has been solved, what will the situation look like?" The miracle question from solution-focused therapy can be useful here. It is "If a miracle happened and your problem was solved, how would your life be different?"[6] It helps to encourage the person to be specific and to dream big. If the language about miracles feels inappropriate to you in this context, you might be playful and ask, "If I waved a magic wand to make it all better, where would you be?" You can also ask something like, "If we were to work together to address your concern fully to your complete satisfaction, where would you be at the end of the work?" You can help people articulate their vision and access their motivation for change by asking for specifics with questions like "How would your life look?" and "What would be different?" and "How would you feel?"

Lastly, you can ask questions to discover difficulties the person has encountered as she has tried to journey on her own from where she is to where she wants to be. Of course, the obvious question is "What difficulties have you run into as you have tried to solve this problem?" Similar questions include "What is blocking you?" "What is getting in the way?" and "What is keeping you stuck?" Additionally, you can ask, "How have you tried to solve this problem?" or "What have you tried?" Hearing about how the person has tried and failed can point out struggles the person is facing.

As you listen to where the person is, where he wants to be, and what blocks he has encountered, you may hear your parishioner expressing some feelings. Remember that the feelings we consider negative are telling us that something needs changing in our lives.[7] For example, when your congregant expresses anger, sadness, or fear, you know that his journey includes the need to change something. In later steps, you will seek to determine appropriate and loving actions in response to the feelings. Right now, in step two, you can pay attention to the expression of feelings as a message about what needs to be changed.

Anger, sadness, and fear all communicate about specific issues that need to be addressed or changed. Andrew Lester said that anger tells us that something important to us has been threatened,[8] while Karla McLaren said that anger tells us that something must be protected or restored.[9] As you attend to the person's journey about where she is, where she wants to be, and what problems she is encountering, anger lets you know that she may be wanting to protect or restore something important to her that is being threatened. McLaren says that the message of sadness is that something must be released or rejuvenated.[10] I would add that sadness might tell us that something must be mourned or grieved. When your parishioners express sadness, you can recognize that they need to mourn, release, or rejuvenate something. Martha Beck reflects that the function of fear is to protect us from danger. She adds that when we are in real immediate peril we need to run from the danger.[11] McLaren says that fear tries to prepare us for novel or dangerous situations that we may face in the future. Fear stops us if we are not prepared in order to help us survive.[12] She also reflects that fear tells us that we need to take action.[13] You can know that when your congregants express fear they need to take action to get out of immediate danger, or they need to prepare to face the situation they fear, perhaps by developing skills, setting boundaries, or taking some other action. Feelings offer important information about your parishioner's journey.

While anger, sadness, and fear give us messages about what needs to be changed in our lives, they can also become complicated or distorted. Intense anger, sadness, and fear can be a sign that you need to refer the person to a therapist. If the intensity or complexity of the situation is outside of your area of competence, referral is indicated.

Remember that this step is not the time to solve the problems or develop a plan of action; it is the time to gain as much clarity as possible about where the person is, where she wants to go, and what problems she is experiencing as she tries to get to where she wants to be. You will have to stay focused on these three issues without getting sidetracked in order to attend to the person's journey in the time available for this step. If you stay focused, you can learn what you need to know in the time that you have.

Topics to Avoid while Attending

To learn what you need to know about the person's journey from where he is to where he wants to be, you must stay tightly focused on this step. Several topics will direct the conversation away from Attending to the Journey. As I have already mentioned, do not get ahead of yourself by seeking answers before you have completed this step and understood the problem. You must also avoid focusing on the past. Questions like "How did this happen?" and "How did you get here?" invite a focus on the past that will spend time you do not have and perhaps move toward a therapeutic approach rather than a ministry focus. In the CARING process you are attending to the journey from the present to a future goal, including the difficulties along the way.

These conversations are derailed by exploring the past, how people got to their current situation. If you want to reflect about the past to understand how it is affecting the person now, you are doing a different kind of ministry. In CARING conversations, issues from the person's past that are relevant to solving the current problem will emerge as you explore the thoughts and feelings that hinder taking the desired actions. Following the CARING process will lead the person toward changes in the present and the future. If the person is unable to make changes after a couple of conversations following the CARING process, she may need more specialized or in-depth help. This inability to make changes could be a sign to consider referring the person to another professional.

Some of your congregants may have been in therapy previously and could try to turn the pastoral conversation toward therapeutic processes or goals. Your job is to clearly define how you are helping them and to be clear about the limits and boundaries of what the CARING process offers. You might need to directly comment that you are seeking to help them determine changes to make without exploring the past like a therapist might. Sometimes you can redirect their focus. For example, after a person has told you what his problem is, he might begin to talk about where it came from. You can gently stop him and say something like, "For this conversation, instead of exploring how you got into this situation, let's talk about what you want for your future. Where would you want to be if the problem were solved?" Given the flow of the conversation, it might be more relevant to ask, "What struggles have you encountered as you have tried to solve this problem?"

Focusing too much on the past and how people got into their problems were mistakes I made many times as I developed and practiced the CARING process. If you find that you have gotten focused on exploring the past rather than following the methodology, you can correct the direction of the conversation. You can say, "Let's shift our attention now to seeking a solution for the problem." If needed, you might say, "Before we move to step three (or start trying to solve the problem), will you summarize in a couple of sentences where you are, where you want to be, and what difficulties you are encountering?" I have found that people are generally able to offer these kinds of summary statements when I request them.

Another topic to avoid is providing answers when people ask you what they should do. Parishioners often give ministers a lot of authority and see us as the people with the answers. They often ask us for advice about all manner of topics about which we may or may not have expertise. Congregants often ask, "What do you think I should do?" It is crucial that you avoid giving people advice when this question is asked. Telling them what to do puts them in the role of dependent child and puts you in the role of authoritative parent. It short-circuits their access to their own inner wisdom and their relationship with God. Advice giving can actually block their access to God. It is wise to facilitate their connection to God and their own wisdom rather than to block it. Steps three through six show you how to facilitate people's connection to God as they seek to solve their problems. Here in step two you simply need to avoid giving advice. When someone asks "What do you think I should do?" you have several options. You might say, "We will explore the question of what you should do a little later in the conversation." You could say, "I want to help you listen to your own wisdom and to God about what you should do. The next step in that direction is..." Then you go back to guiding the person through the CARING process, picking up where you left off.

Sometimes congregants ask, "In your professional opinion, what should I do?" With this question, they are asking us to accept the role of authority with the answers. This question exerts subtle pressure, as if saying, "This is what I expect of you as my minister" or "If you were a good pastoral care provider, you would give me your professional opinion."

I have found it helpful when I am tempted to assume the role of professional authority to remember the discussions by Henri Nouwen and Parker Palmer of the temptations of Jesus. Nouwen teaches that the temptations were to be relevant ("turn these stones to bread"), spectacular ("throw yourself down"), and powerful ("I will give you all").[14] "If you are the son of God you will do this" is not so different from "If you are a good minister you will do this." The temptation to try to prove our worthiness, relevance, power, or special abilities can be very strong. As Palmer reflects, "The root temptation here is almost irresistible. It is not the temptation to do a magic trick, which most of us know we cannot. It is the temptation to prove our identity, which many of us feel we must."[15] We can combat it as Jesus did. Palmer describes Jesus's response to these temptations as follows: "He knows that right action does not require us to be relevant, powerful, or spectacular. Right action requires only that we respond faithfully to our own inner truth and to the truth around us. It requires not that we aim at any particular outcome, for ourselves or for others, but that we act on truth as we know it, with truth as our only end."[16] Nouwen suggests that we can combat the temptation to relevance with prayer.[17] He also reflects that we can fight the temptation to be spectacular by seeking to move from popularity to ministry.[18] Finally, Nouwen recommends overcoming the temptation to be powerful by moving from leading to being led.[19] Rather than succumbing to these temptations, we can seek to be authentic, realistic, and humble.

When parishioners ask for our professional opinions, we must remember that we are spiritual guides, not God. We choose to believe that facilitating spiritual growth is more important than giving expected answers that are not helpful. We can respond, "I will help you listen to God about this" and "What your own inner wisdom says about this question is more important than my ideas. I can help you listen to your higher self."

In a similar way, individuals may want to ask your opinion about areas that are outside of your expertise, such as legal, business, or financial matters. The same temptations and responses can happen with those questions. In addition to guiding the person to listen to God and her own inner wisdom, you can also guide her to find qualified people to address her needs.

Pitfalls to Avoid while Attending

Throughout step two, there are a few pitfalls to avoid as you are attending to the journey. Do not try to solve the parishioner's problem, or even to guide him to solve it at this stage of the conversation. That work comes later. Do not try to change thoughts, feelings, or actions in order to change results. At this point, you are simply seeking to understand. Later you will facilitate problem-solving, shifts, and change. At this step you want to deepen the understanding of the problem for yourself and your parishioner. You want to finish Attending to the Journey with clarity about three things: where the person is, what struggles he is encountering, and where he wants to be.

Assess the Need

Thus far, my discussion of Attending to the Journey has assumed that the person is addressing an issue that is appropriate for pastoral problem-solving conversations. When people come to you for help, they are seeking relief or assistance, and it is your job to determine what kind of help their situation requires. Once you have invited them to tell you what their problem is, you will actually need to be listening on two levels. One level is Attending to the Journey, as I have already discussed. Another level is Assess the Need, or determining what kind of ministry is necessary.

After you have asked the person to tell you about her problem, as you attend to her journey, you should also notice what kind of issue she is bringing to you and what kind of help she needs from you. Issues that are appropriate for CARING conversations include solving problems, reaching goals, and growing personally or spiritually. In these instances the CARING process is appropriate and you should continue with it. At other times, people come to you seeking education or information related to your church or organization. If people are asking to be taught something or to be provided information, trying to help them find the answers within themselves is not effective or necessary. Sometimes ministers can be so happy to have experienced the effectiveness of the

CARING process that they begin to apply it in situations better suited to other types of ministry. If a parishioner is asking for education, then you can simply offer information appropriate to your ministry role, or you can refer her to the correct person within the organization.

If a parishioner is struggling with a painful life situation she may need for you to provide the ministry of presence, representing the sustaining love of God in the midst of her situation. If so, use your pastoral care knowledge and skills to walk alongside the person as she struggles. If this kind of ministry is difficult for you, you can find help from pastoral educators from the Association for Clinical Pastoral Education, therapists, or spiritual guides, as well as the literature of pastoral care.

In these ministry encounters, you will need to discern whether the situation calls for pastoral presence, a CARING pastoral conversation, or both. Obviously, the first step of CARING does bring presence and connection to conversations. In making this distinction, you will need to consider your own inner wisdom. What is the most loving choice? What does your inner wisdom tell you about what is needed? When I want to check my motivation, I find the following questions helpful: "Am I wanting to move into problem-solving as a way to avoid being present with pain and suffering?" and "Am I choosing a ministry of presence because I don't believe that solutions can be discovered?" You can ask your parishioner for her wisdom about what she needs from you. Of course, you can also ask God for guidance. With practice, your process of discernment will become more clear.

If at any point you realize that this situation is a crisis, you need to shift immediately into crisis ministry, using the principles and skills offered in the pastoral care literature. If the situation is not a crisis but it calls for help outside your area of expertise, it is wise to refer. Mental health issues should be referred to a therapist. Physical health issues should be referred to a doctor. Legal or financial concerns should be referred to the appropriate professional. The pastoral care literature offers guidance about crisis ministry, when and how to refer, the reasons to refer, and good pastoral care practices in referring. If you are not skilled in crisis ministry and referral, please review this literature and practice these concepts or invest in continuing education on this topic.

Years ago, Wayne Oates dubbed referral "the ministry of introduction" in his book *The Christian Pastor*.[20] This concept is a useful framework as you follow the guidance for making referrals in the current pastoral care literature. You are providing significant ministry when you introduce parishioners to persons who can help them with their specific concerns. You can reassure people that you will continue to have a ministry relationship with them, even as they receive help from other professionals. You will continue to be their pastor and to provide spiritual care.

Pitfalls to Avoid while Assessing the Need

A few issues should be avoided as you are assessing what kind of help the person needs. First, do not fall into the trap of providing the same kind of help for every problem, whether it is a CARING conversation, providing information, offering the ministry of presence, or treating every issue as a crisis. Make distinctions and assess what kind of help is needed for each particular person who requests your assistance with each specific situation.

Second, do not believe that you must be relevant, spectacular, and powerful in all of your ministry conversations. Closely related to this one is the belief that you must do everything people ask of you and that you are the one who must solve every problem. Remember that your job is to guide the conversation, to ask powerful questions, and to facilitate your parishioner's connection with God and inner wisdom. It is the person's job to answer the questions, seek guidance within and from God, and to make a plan of action.

Sometimes your congregants will not want to accept your referrals, insisting that you are the only one who can help them. Because you care, you can be tempted to try to help with issues that are beyond your expertise. This is where the deep meaning of "love your neighbor as you love yourself" (Matt 22:39) comes into play. To meet the standard of Christlike love, any action should be loving to both yourself and your neighbors. When you do what is loving and right for yourself, you will stay within the boundaries of your skill and knowledge. Doing so is loving for your parishioners also. You invite them to seek help from the appropriate professional person who can offer specialized assistance. Both you and your congregants will benefit from your keeping these boundaries in place. I believe that as we pray "forgive us our trespasses" (Matt 6:9-13) we are reminded not to enter territory that is not ours.[21] When you are tempted to function outside the boundaries of your skill and knowledge, you might offer a prayer for help to avoid trespassing.

Integrating Previous Steps and Ongoing Use of This Step

As you attend to the person's journey and assess what kind of help is needed, you will want to stay connected with yourself, the other person, and God. You have to be connected to your own inner wisdom for both attending to the journey and assessing the need. You also must be connected to your higher self to avoid the temptations that arise when people ask for your help in solving their problems. Your connection with God, praying silently as needed, will also help you avoid these temptations. You will also, of course, maintain a pastoral relationship with the other person. Pay attention to how he responds to you and use your skills to continue the helping relationship.

An ongoing use of Attend to the Journey and Assess the Need will support the rest of the conversation. Sometimes, later in the conversation, people will add or change information about where they are, problems they are facing, and where they want to be. If you continue listening for these key factors, you will hear important and helpful information about the situation as you lead the next steps of the pastoral conversation. Depending on exactly what is said, you might just need to notice it, you might need to ask for clarification, or it could be necessary to renegotiate the problem you have agreed to work on together.

Later in the conversation, you might be given information that changes your assessment of the type of help that is needed. Sometimes you begin the CARING process in good faith, believing that it is the best way to help the person, but as the conversation goes on, the person expresses concerns that let you know a different type of ministry would be more appropriate for the situation. When you make that assessment, simply shift to the type of ministry that is appropriate to the person's need.

How to Know You Have Completed This Step

You are ready to move to the third step of the CARING process when you have completed all of the following actions.

- You have assessed what kind of help is needed and decided that a CARING conversation is appropriate.

- You have attended to where he is.

- You have attended to the difficulties he has experienced.

- You have attended to where he wants to be.

- You have asked questions to clarify any issues you do not understand.

- You have led him to discuss all three aspects of the journey (where he is, difficulties, and where he wants to be).

- You have asked about thoughts, feelings, and actions.

- You will not have asked about other matters, such as how he got to where he is, that you are curious about but which take time and energy away from the CARING process.

- If you did make this mistake, you corrected it when you noticed it, and you asked for at least a summary statement of where he is, where he wants to be, and the blocks to reaching that goal.

- You feel confident that you understand the person's journey.

- You could summarize each of the three aspects of the journey in a single sentence.

This clarity about the journey helps you be ready to move on to the third step, which will be discussed in the next chapter.

Chapter Three

STEP 3: REACH CLARITY ABOUT THE REALISTIC FOCUS FOR THIS CONVERSATION

This chapter is about the third step of the CARING process: Reach Clarity about the Realistic Focus for This Conversation. This step naturally follows the previous one. Once you and your parishioner are clear about where she is, the difficulties she faces, and where she wants to be, then inviting your parishioner to determine a focus for this conversation is a natural and logical progression. In terms of the time frame for the conversation, you should aim to be finished with step three when roughly half of the time for the conversation has passed. For a thirty-minute conversation, you should aim to complete step three at around the fifteen-minute mark. For an hour-long conversation, you would aim to complete step three by the thirty-minute mark. With a longer conversation, it can be helpful to leave additional time for the later steps if these first three can be accomplished more quickly without overlooking any important information. Another consideration regarding time is that the goal for the conversation

47

will need to be small enough to complete in the time you have left for the conversation. This chapter will address how to develop a realistic focus for the conversation.

How a Clear Focus Helps

This step is the heart of the CARING process. When it is done well, the rest of the conversation will flow smoothly. When a realistic focus for the conversation is clearly defined, people will find inspiration for actions that will help them meet their goals. You will have clear parameters for the conversation with an agreed-upon focus for the conversation. You will have a touchstone to come back to if you lose your way in later steps as you are guiding the conversation. If you get lost, it is very helpful to say, "The focus for our conversation is *this* (repeat it). We can move toward it by doing *this*." Here you name the step you need to complete or are ready to move toward. On the other hand, if a realistic focus is not clearly delineated, the conversation may flounder as you continue. Be sure to give careful attention to a well-defined goal for the conversation.

The importance of having a realistic focus for a pastoral conversation can be extrapolated from the definition of *focus* in *The Coach U Personal and Corporate Coach Training Handbook*: "As a noun, a focus is the central point of attraction, attention, or activity. As a verb, to focus means to concentrate on something as the central point, freeing self of distractions or other outside influence that would confuse whatever is the point of attraction."[1]

A well-defined, realistic focus gives you and your parishioner an important point of attention to be used throughout the conversation. It is a clear destination for the conversation, which will help you immensely. If at any time you lose your way, you can return to the goal for the conversation. If you follow the six steps, the parishioner will develop a plan of action to lead him toward this goal by the end of the conversation.

A clear focus also primes the pump for problem solving, which comes next in the CARING process. Human beings have great capacity for puzzle-solving and problem-solving. When we clearly name a problem, an area of focus, it is as if we give our entire being instructions to solve the problem, according to James Loder's *The Transforming Moment*.[2] Often when parishioners clarify *this* is the small, specific, realistic problem I want to address in today's conversation, they immediately are inspired with a solution or a plan. This inspiration does not seem to come from simply sharing their concerns with someone who is attending to their journey. Sharing the journey and then saying *this* is the problem I want to solve in this conversation almost invariably leads to the person coming up with an answer or a step in the right direction. Inspired answers often follow the statement of the focus or goal for the conversation.

Reach Clarity

A clear focus will help you and your parishioner. It is important that you guide your parishioner to discern a goal for the conversation. The mnemonic for step three begins with the phrase "reach clarity" to indicate that you and your parishioner will work together to develop a clear and realistic goal for the conversation. The focus should be a realistic next step toward solving the problem or addressing the concern. It should be easy to address the goal in the time you have left for the conversation. A realistic focus is often the first step that the person needs to take to solve the problem. An effective focus for the ministry conversation will narrow the gap between where the person is and where she wants to be. Well-defined goals are realistic, small, and focused enough to be completed in the time you have left in the conversation.

Helpful goals for a pastoral conversation have several characteristics. They are often about removing blocks or accessing resources. Both of these processes help people solve problems or reach goals. Good goals are about what the person you are ministering with can do; they are not about what the person wants someone else to do. A helpful goal for a ministry conversation will facilitate the person to move toward Christlike love, truth, and freedom rather than away from these qualities. Meaningful goals will be congruent with the person's spirituality and moral values.

How to Develop Good Goals

You begin the process of reaching agreement about the area of focus for the conversation by telling the person that you will now work together to choose the goal for this conversation. I find it useful to ask the person for his ideas. I often begin by asking, "What do you want to get out of this conversation?" or using one of John Patton's magic questions, "What are you looking for?"[3] I often choose to be even more specific by asking, "When we have finished this conversation, what do you want to have happened? What do you want to take with you when you leave?"

Many times, a parishioner can name a clear goal for the conversation in response to these questions. Sometimes he has already named a possible goal at the very beginning of the conversation or during step two, Attend to the Journey and Assess the Need. A congregant might simply repeat the goal in response to these questions, or you might remind him of the goal he described earlier. Here is an instance where keeping brief notes can help you, if you have written down any goals mentioned during the first two steps.

When a parishioner gives you clear goals for the conversation that you believe are realistic and will help her, you can agree with the goal, perhaps suggesting small adjustments to improve its effectiveness. After telling her that you believe the goal will help her, repeat it back to her, saying something like, "The goal for this conversation will be *this*." Then ask for her agreement ("Do you agree?" or "Have I accurately understood what you want to do?") and write down the goal. You will use this clear area of focus for the rest of the conversation.

Many times, choosing and assessing a goal will be this simple. If you have a clear focus quickly, be grateful and move on to step four. You will find that you can make good use of the time you did not need for this step on future ones.

When a congregant has difficulty choosing a goal for the pastoral conversation, he will need some additional guidance from you. Generally a goal is more effective if it emerges from the person seeking help. Do not give up too soon on helping the person access his inner wisdom. You can ask, "What ideas do you have?" and "What else?" to help him explore his hopes for the conversation. Another question that helps people choose a realistic goal is "What does the wisest part of you see as the most helpful thing for us to address today?" If it seems appropriate to the relationship and context you can pray together for God's help in choosing an area of focus for the conversation. Even with this guidance, a person might continue to struggle to develop a goal for the conversation. In such cases, using the information in the rest of this chapter will help you guide step three effectively.

When the Person Has Difficulty Choosing a Goal

As you are seeking to reach clarity about a realistic focus for this conversation, your parishioner might struggle to develop a purpose for the conversation. If the person has difficulty choosing a goal, you can suggest some possible ideas for consideration as the focus for the conversation. Here is where you make use of the information you gathered as you were attending to the person's journey. Of course you can remind the congregant of any goals you heard as you listened to his story, and ask if any of them would be a good realistic focus for the conversation. If not, you have other options. Three possible areas of focus often emerge from Attending to the Journey: removing blocks to progress, accessing resources that can assist progress, and hearing and responding to the messages of feelings.

Remove Blocks

An extremely effective way of choosing a goal in step three is to create a goal that focuses on removing something that blocks the person's progress. From listening well to the stories of the person's journey, you will have a clear sense of the struggles that are stopping her from moving from where she is to where she wants to be. As part of attending to her journey, you listened for thoughts that led to feelings that led to actions that led to results.[4] When people are not achieving the outcomes they desire, then thoughts, feelings, or actions might be blocks for them. If this is the case, a helpful goal would be to change the thoughts, feelings, or actions. You might be aware of problems with thoughts, feelings, actions, or all three. You can share this observation with the person, suggesting that changing thoughts, feelings, actions, or all three experiences would be a helpful goal for the conversation.

If you can guide your parishioner to find a way to remove a difficulty, then he will be free to move toward his goal. A person who is struggling with a block to a goal is like someone who is trying to drive with one foot on the accelerator and another foot on the brake. If you help him take his foot off the brake, he will have more momentum and make more progress toward his destination. You might say to the person, "As I listened to you, it sounded like *this* (give specifics) is the main issue that is stopping you from reaching your goal. We could consider overcoming that struggle as a possible focus for this conversation." If the issue is too much to address in the time you have left in the conversation, ask, "What part of that struggle would you like to deal with today?"

Sometimes blocks cannot be removed but must instead be worked around. One of my doctor of ministry students includes a helpful analogy for this situation in his project thesis. A difficulty can be like a really big stump in the way of a farmer plowing a field. To remove it would cost more time and money than the farmer has available. Instead of working to remove the block, the farmer simply plows around it.[5] With some people, you might tell that story and then say, "From listening to your story, I would say that *this* (give specifics) is an obstacle that is too costly and difficult to remove. We could choose to focus this conversation on helping you find a way to navigate (or plow, if the farming metaphor works for the person) around it."

Access Resources

If navigating around blocks is like plowing around a big stump, then accessing resources is like using a tractor rather than a plow to do the job. If overcoming obstacles is like taking your foot off the brake when it is there unnecessarily, then accessing resources is like pushing the accelerator when needed although you have been avoiding doing so. Accessing resources can be a focus for the pastoral conversation that helps your parishioner go around obstacles and move toward his goal.

You might be aware of resources your congregant is missing or not using in his quest to get to where he wants to be. Your parishioner might not be connecting with God, his own higher wisdom, or other people, so developing a plan to do so will help him reach where he wants to be in his journey. Sometimes the person may need to do further research before the next steps become clear to him, and figuring out how to do so can be a goal of the conversation.

Hear and Respond to the Messages of Feelings

A final way to guide your parishioner to choose a goal is to invite her to listen to the messages of her feelings. You will have noticed feelings as you were attending to the parishioner's journey. If your congregant expressed feelings that indicated immediate danger, you will have already instituted crisis ministry, and if she expressed feelings that indicated mental illness, a danger to herself or others, or issues that call for therapy, you will have referred her for appropriate professional help.

Therefore, the feelings discussed here are not those that indicate a need for crisis ministry or therapeutic referral, but are the feelings that people who are not in crisis or mentally ill might experience. If your parishioner expressed sadness in telling you about her journey, a pastoral goal might be reflecting on what needs mourning, releasing, or rejuvenating[6] and making a plan about how to do so. If your congregant expressed fear about a possible new situation that feels threatening, then a pastoral goal might be to figure out how to prepare for the new situation, or to explore what action needs to be taken.[7] If the person expressed anger about something important being threatened, then the pastoral goal might be addressing the questions "What do I want to protect?" and "What needs to be restored?"[8] and making a plan to protect or restore the valuable thing.

In step three the feelings can be used to help you and your parishioner reach clarity about a realistic focus for this conversation. If you go this route in choosing a goal, you will address the pastoral questions for feelings in step four, rather than as part of step three. The purpose of the third step is simply choosing a realistic goal for the conversation, such as discovering what must be protected and making a plan to take care of this significant thing. Then in the rest of the pastoral conversation, you will guide the person to reach the goal you have agreed upon for this conversation.

Assess the Chosen Goal

When your parishioner has offered a possible goal for the conversation, you can help him determine if this area of focus is realistic. You might ask, "Can we reach this goal in the time we have left for this conversation?" Often I find that people want to begin with large goals. Sometimes people will name five things that they want to accomplish by the end of the conversation. To help them get to a more realistic goal, you can then say something like "You have named these things that you want to accomplish (repeat the list). Those are all important. We have time to address one goal today. Where would you like to start?"

My experience is that people are able to answer this question quickly and easily. Most persons seem to have clarity as I ask where they want to start. Sometimes individuals say that they want to start with one particular goal because it needs to be done first before the others can be addressed. Some people say that they want to start with an easier goal to give them some momentum. Other persons say that they want my help with the most difficult goal so that once they have tackled it the rest of the process will be easier. My parishioners very often answer this question with both a goal and a reason for their choice.

Even when people choose one goal, it is very often still too large to productively address in the fifteen to thirty minutes that are typically left in a ministry conversation once you have chosen an area of focus. When the person's goal is too large to be realistic, you might ask the question, "What part of *that* do you want to work on?" Keep asking the question, "What part of that do you want to work on?" Sometimes it will take as many as four or five times until the goal is specific, focused, and realistic.

You can use other questions to guide your parishioner to assess if he has chosen a helpful goal for the conversation. Will it help him move toward Christlike love or away from it? You can ask your congregant this question directly. Of course, you might ask a similar question, using language that will be familiar to your congregant. You could also ask, "Is our focus for this conversation loving, mature, and true?" or "Is this goal loving to yourself, other people, and God?"

Sometimes people do try to choose goals that are not congruent with their own wisdom or best interests. I learned this lesson from observing a spiritual coach working with a client. The client asked this coach for help in working smarter to meet some goals at her job. If I had been the coach I would have agreed that this goal was a realistic focus for a coaching conversation. The response of the more-experienced coach stunned me. She said, "You are already working too much and too hard. I do not want to help you work even more. That will not help you. It will hurt you." This feedback was delivered in a direct, matter-of-fact, and compassionate tone. The client laughed ruefully and agreed with her coach's feedback. They chose a goal more in line with the client's deeper needs for attending to her health and well-being.

Likewise, you can give your parishioners direct, matter-of-fact, and compassionate feedback about their goals for pastoral conversations. You might want to offer them feedback when you believe that their goals are not congruent with their spirituality or will be detrimental to their growth. When offering challenging responses, it is important to do so with an attitude of humility and respect for your parishioner.

You might also ask the questions, "Will this goal improve your spiritual growth?" and "Is it congruent with your spirituality as a follower of Christ?" You might more simply ask, "Will this goal help you be more loving?" If the goal is not congruent with your congregant's spirituality, you can follow up by asking, "How can you modify your goal to help you grow toward love?" or "If we listen to God and to the wisest part of you, what goals might they suggest for this conversation?"

If the person continues to struggle to answer these questions, he is experiencing a block to his journey in the conversation itself.

You could ask, "Is there something that is stopping you from having a goal that helps you move toward more love?" or "What is blocking you from moving in the direction you want to go?" Naming the struggle that is occurring within the pastoral conversation can help people to form a realistic goal for the CARING process. At these times, navigating around this block might become the goal of the conversation.

Conclude This Step

After you have decided upon a goal, make sure that you state it clearly and ask for the person's agreement. Say something like, "The goal we will work on for this conversation is *this*. Did I understand you correctly? Do you agree to that goal for this conversation?" It is also helpful at this point to write it down, so that you can keep returning to the goal as necessary throughout the rest of the conversation.

Pitfalls to Avoid

Three pitfalls are important to avoid. The most common is agreeing to work on a goal that is too large in scope. Choosing a goal that is not realistic for the time you have remaining for the conversation is setting yourself up to be less effective than you could be. Both you and your parishioner will tend to flounder and feel overwhelmed if the goal is too large. An area of focus that is undefined or too large will not do its job of providing clarity for the conversation and inspiring your parishioner to develop a loving action plan.

It is definitely better to err on the side of being too small and too focused than to allow a large and unfocused goal. If your goal is small and tightly focused, you might finish early. Do not feel that you must fill the time. If the person has created a defined action plan with clear steps, it is better to conclude early than to risk overwhelming the parishioner with too much information. On the other hand, you might finish quickly with a small plan and feel that your congregant could benefit from additional work. In this case, you can go back to step three and choose an area of focus that can be addressed in the time you have left.

A technique I have found helpful to get to a realistic goal is to keep using the question "What part of *that* do you want to work on?" You can ask that question a number of times until the person becomes unable to narrow the focus to a smaller goal. With practice you will begin to recognize when goals are small enough to be realistic.

Remember, Jesus valued small things. Do not worry that the goal is too small. Mustard seeds (Matt 13:31) and yeast (Matt 13:33) are small things that produce significant results. One of my teachers used to say that changing a rocket's trajectory by only a few degrees would make a significant difference in the rocket's destination. In the same way, when human beings make small changes, the results are often significant.

A second pitfall to avoid is the trap of trying to be the expert. You can avoid this one when you remind your congregants that they are the experts of their own lives and that you will help them to discover what they already know or to listen to God and their own inner wisdom. Your job is to ask powerful questions and to guide the conversation so that your parishioners find their own answers by encountering God and their higher selves. Your task is not to be the expert with the answers or to be God!

Doubting the person's inner wisdom and connection with God becomes a third pitfall to guard against. With a person who does not often demonstrate wisdom, it is easy to fall into the trap of believing that you have to fix her and tell her what to do. With a complex problem, you may feel discouraged or doubt her ability to be creative or inspired. Keep the faith. Believe in your parishioner's resources. Trust that she knows more about her life and problem than you do. Believe that if you follow the CARING process her wisdom will emerge. People in very difficult circumstances can access their wisdom and connection with God when ministers invite them to do so.

Integrating Previous Steps and Ongoing Use of This Step

Staying connected will help both you and your parishioner to decide upon a helpful focus for the conversation. You will also want to continue to pay attention to what your congregant tells you about where he is, where he wants to be, and the difficulties he is experiencing. As he seeks a realistic focus, you may learn more about his journey that will help you facilitate his growth and change throughout the process.

You will continue using the realistic focus you have agreed upon through the rest of the conversation. This goal gives you a topic to address in a single-minded way. You can restate the goal to bring the conversation back to focus whenever you or your parishioner become distracted. You will work toward reaching the goal for this pastoral conversation in the next three steps of the CARING process.

Blending Steps Two and Three

I once worked with a very effective coach who approached this issue a little differently than I do. She blended steps two and three. She listened carefully, but was willing to suggest possible areas of focus. For example, when I described my situation and concerns, if she heard something that sounded like a meaningful focus, she often asked, "Is that something you want to focus on today?" Often she added, "Or do you have something more urgent you wanted?" Especially when time is short, this approach could be beneficial for ministers.

The Hourglass Image

Coaches often use the image of an hourglass to picture a coaching conversation. The conversation is like the flow of the sand through an hourglass. When you turn a full hourglass over, the sand at the top of the hourglass is like the beginning of the conversation. It is a wide start. Connecting to God, self, and others is a wide beginning. As the sand flows down the hourglass, the conversation becomes more narrowly focused. You are attending only to where the person is, where she wants to be, and what struggles she is experiencing. This is a medium-wide topic. It is more focused than connecting, but less so than reaching clarity about a goal for the conversation. As the sand flows from top to bottom, it reaches a place where it is flowing slowly through the narrowest part of the hourglass. That space is like choosing an area of focus for a pastoral conversation. Slowing down and making the choice of a realistic focus for the conversation carefully will help you reach clarity about a goal that is small, narrow, and realistic.

At the end of step three, you have completed the first half of the conversation. When you move to step four, it is as if you have turned the hourglass over and you begin seeking to reach your goal in a way that is wide. The conversation will once again narrow further in step five and then come to a small, focused action plan in step six.

How to Know You Have Completed This Step

When you have accomplished the following activities, you have finished this step and are ready to move to the next one.

- You have asked the person what he wants to focus on.
- You have helped him narrow it down to a realistic goal that will work in the time frame of the conversation.
- If you were not sure the goal is small enough, you asked, "What part of *that* would you like to work on today?"
- You repeated the question "What part of *that*?" until the goal felt realistic and reachable.
- You have assessed that the goal is congruent with his spirituality.
- You have stated the goal.
- You have asked for agreement.
- You have written it down.

You are now ready to move to step four and begin the second half of the process, which will seek to meet the goal you have set together for this pastoral conversation.

Chapter Four

STEP 4: INSPIRE THE DEVELOPMENT OF A LOVING ACTION PLAN

The next step of the process of conducting pastoral conversations is to Inspire the Development of a Loving Action Plan. You do this by inviting help from God, the person's higher self, and other people as you search for possibilities to reach the goal you have set. You invite the person to seek solutions for the problem, possibilities, answers, and options. At this point, you want to assume that there are numerous ways to solve the problem and that inspiration is available.

In terms of the hourglass image, the first half of the conversation followed the sands trickling from broadest to narrowest. In this step, it is as if you have turned the hourglass over for the second half of the conversation. In step four, you broaden the conversation again, seeking help from God, your higher selves, and other resources. Together you will brainstorm solutions to the goal you have chosen for the conversation. In later steps you will narrow the discussion to developing a specific action plan. Just as the first step was about connecting to God, self, and others to understand the problem, this step that begins the second half of the ministry conversation seeks resources from these sources of wisdom to help solve the problem. Step four is about a wide search for solutions.

You should move to this step immediately after choosing the goal for the conversation. I usually conclude the previous step by saying something like, "OK, the goal for our conversation is *this...*" Sometimes the person begins to brainstorm answers immediately. At other times, you will need to direct the person to the fourth step.

When the Congregant Creates a Plan Immediately after Clarifying the Focus

Often, once I have stated the goal, the congregant will say something like, "Well, here's how I could go about doing *that...*" Fairly frequently, the person names three to five steps he can take to reach the goal. I believe that inspiration emerges precisely because we have carefully attended to his situation and have chosen where to start in solving the problem. As the late James Loder, philosophy of Christian education professor at Princeton Theological Seminary, teaches in his book *The Transforming Moment*, when we experience a puzzle or conflict, "we tend to want to set it right or to know that it is all right that it not be settled."[1] Loder additionally postulates, "To be temporarily baffled over a conflict in one's situation is to be drawn both consciously and unconsciously into the familiar psychological process of searching out the possible solutions, taking apart errors, keeping parts, and discarding others."[2]

In other words, once a conflict is engaged, the human spirit begins searching for resolution. In steps two and three of the CARING process, you engage the conflict, inviting the person to explore the puzzle in his life. By guiding these steps, you have already begun inspiring the development of an action plan. Step four continues this work deliberately.

Having a clear starting place and problem to solve ends the congregant's overwhelmed feeling and often leads to startling clarity. Parishioners often name significant actions they could take as soon as you reach this step. It is important that you capture these ideas, preferably in writing. You can make notes on paper or ask your parishioner to jot down the action items. You might even use a whiteboard as you talk to capture the inspired ideas that emerge. If you are not making notes, carefully pay attention so that you will remember these ideas.

While your parishioner is inspired, it is useful to invite her to continue exploring solutions. After she has named a few spontaneously, you might simply ask, "What else comes to mind?" or "What other ideas do you have?" Keep asking questions like this until the person has completed the initial statement of inspired ideas.

If, as you are hearing your congregant's ideas, you begin to feel inspired as well, it is appropriate to share your thoughts with him. Do so with humility, remembering that he is the expert on his own life and that your ideas might not work for him. In my experience, inspiration will feel light, and I will not feel attached to the outcome. It is as if my thought is "Hmm, that is an idea that might work." There is no hint of desperation or feeling that I must make something happen or fix the problem for the person.

Sometimes ideas are discovered in the dialogue between minister and parishioner. It can look like this: the parishioner says, "I could do this and that." The minister is inspired by something the parishioner has said and then adds, "Or you could do this other thing." The parishioner might say, "No, that won't work because... But that makes me think of this. What a great idea." Possibilities are discovered in the give-and-take of a pastoral conversation.

At times the action plan may feel complete after this initial discussion of possible ideas. If so, then move on to step five. If you want to develop the action plan further, or if the congregant did not immediately offer solutions, continue by using the instructions in the rest of this chapter.

Introduce This Step

When the immediate ideas have been offered, or if your congregant did not spontaneously suggest solutions or actions, you will guide her to consciously invite help and search for solutions. You do so by a brief comment to guide her into step four. You might say something like, "We will now begin the process of focusing on (name the area of focus). We are seeking to find an answer for that problem. We will look for help from God, our higher wisdom, and other resources to help you develop a loving action plan." Sometimes ministers find it helpful to pray at this point in the conversation. At other times, especially when step one has included praying for God's help, another prayer at this step may feel repetitive or unnecessary. Use your best judgment based on the content of the conversation and your own spiritual discernment.

If the person has spontaneously offered some ideas, you might say something like, "Your own higher self has already offered us some wisdom. It seems like talking about the problem and deciding where to start activated your own inner wisdom." If she did not spontaneously begin to problem-solve, you might ask, "Are there any ideas that have come to mind for you since we have explored the problem and decided where to start?"

Loder indicates that at some point in the inward and outward scanning for possibilities, an "aha" moment will emerge in which the person recognizes an answer to his dilemma. Loder suggests that this insight occurs because of a "constructive act of the imagination."[3] The insight includes a "release of the energy bound up in sustaining the conflict and an opening of the knower to himself or herself and the contextual situation."[4] When the "aha" moment appears, the person is ready to develop an action plan. Sometimes this happens as soon as a focused goal for the conversation is chosen, as has already been discussed, and you might then invite the person to develop an action plan based on this new insight.

At other times the "aha" emerges as you guide the person to listen to her own inner wisdom, God, and the wisdom of other people. Watch for and notice the "aha" moments as you guide the person through this step. They often provide insights that will help your parishioner form an action plan. Ask about (and write down) action steps after you have noticed an "aha" experience from your parishioner.

In introducing step four to your congregant, you may also use the concept of brainstorming, which is a way of thinking of many possibilities to address the goal for the conversation. People come up with more and better solutions if they remember not to evaluate or censor them at first. You simply capture them, preferably in writing. You might say to your parishioner that as you are look-ing for solutions you will brainstorm together. Remind him that brainstorming means that you do not evaluate ideas that emerge, you are simply listing possibilities. Clarify that after you have re-corded possibilities, then you will evaluate them and develop an action plan.

Listen to God, Self, and Others

You will guide the person to listen to God, to her own higher self, and the wisdom of other people, and perhaps also share your ideas. Drawing upon these three sources of wisdom can be done in any order. You can decide what order to use based on the specifics of the focus, the flow of the conversation thus far, and your sense of what order would work best with this particular person in this particular conversation. This discussion begins with listening to the person's higher self because that is usually the most common or logical place to begin this step. It is, of course, where people begin when they spontaneously offer solutions to the problem.

Listen to Self

Invite help from the person's higher self. Invite the person to share insights or inspirations that emerge regarding the spe-cific focus of the conversation. You might ask, "What does the highest, wisest part of you advise to help you move toward your goal?" or "What does the most loving part of you want to do?" One of my coaches used to ask me, "If you knew you could not fail what would you do?" Ask one or more of these questions, listen well, and add the person's answers to the list you are mak-ing of possibilities.

These three queries would be considered powerful questions by personal and corporate coaches. Coach U describes "powerful questioning" as "the ability to ask questions that reveal the information needed for maximum benefits." Coach U lists four functions of powerful questions: (1) they demonstrate an understanding of the person's situation and beliefs; (2) they "evoke discovery, insight, commitment, or action"; (3) they "create greater clarity, possibility, or new learning"; and (4) they "move the coachee toward what he or she desires."[5]

Suzanne Goebel, president of the On Purpose Group, in her *Introduction to Professional Coaching*, lists several examples of powerful questions. Two of her favorites are "How can I be most useful to you during this conversation?" and "What do you need right now?"[6] Other questions Goebel recommends include the following:

- What have you done thus far?
- What are you thinking about as a next step?
- What consequences might there be?
- What other options are you considering?
- What resources will you need to accomplish the task?
- Who can you talk to about this?
- How might you compensate for the risks?[7]

Other powerful questions might be used here as well. In my years of gleaning and acquiring experience, some of the origins of these questions have been obscured from my recall.[8] Here are some that I would suggest:

- What might you try?
- What else? (you might ask this question several times)

- Here is an idea I have. How does it sound to you?
- How have you solved similar problems in the past?
- What has worked for you in similar situations?
- How do you _____ in general?
- Where can you go to find the information you need?

As always, adapt these questions to your own style and the relationship and the situation. You might come up with some questions that are even better. Asking powerful questions is perhaps the easiest and most natural thing for ministers to do in helping their congregants discover their own inner wisdom.

Finally, you can assist people to recognize their own wisdom by using the pastoral questions for feelings described previously. As a reminder, the pastoral questions for anger include "What is the threat?"[9] "What must be protected?" and "What must be restored?"[10] The pastoral questions for sadness include "What needs to be released?" "What needs to be rejuvenated?"[11] and "What must be grieved?" When fear is a response to an immediate and real danger, the necessary action is to run away from danger.[12] If the fear is a response to a possible future situation that would be new or dangerous, the pastoral questions include "How do you need to prepare for this situation you may face in the future?" and "What action needs to be taken?"[13]

Listen to God

In step four, you assist your parishioner in listening for God's wisdom concerning solutions to his problem. You will guide your parishioner through either a spiritual conversation, spiritual practices, or both, that are designed to help him seek and hear God's guidance regarding his concern. You will want to tailor this guidance with the theology and practices that are appropriate for your situation and the person with whom you are ministering. As you turn to this part of the dialogue, be sensitive to the person's context, theology, and relationship with God, or lack of same.

Just as you used powerful questions to help the person listen to her own inner wisdom, you can also use powerful questions to help people listen to God. Numerous quality questions can be used to invite your parishioner to listen to God. One powerful question to invoke while listening to God is "If you had the capacity to behave in the most loving way possible—and I mean loving for everyone concerned, including yourself and God—what would you do?" Another inspiring question for this portion of the pastoral conversation is "If you knew you could not fail at giving and receiving love, at learning to love yourself, God, and the other people involved, what would you do?" Another great spiritual question is "In the situation we are discussing, how might the God of Love help you know what to do?"

You could also very directly ask, "What do you think God is leading you to do?" If the person has an image of God that is tyrannical or that falls short of the touchstone "God is love" (1 John 4:8), you might phrase the question in a way that will help him listen to the Spirit of love who loves him. You might say something like, "Remember that God loves you completely, unconditionally, and extravagantly, and that God wants the best for you. What might the God of love want for you in this situation? What solutions might God offer you?" You could simplify this to the question "What does God's unconditional love want you to know?"

Use your own language and context. Formulate some questions that you can use at this point in the conversation. If you already have a pastoral relationship with the parishioner and have guided his spiritual growth in the past, you will be able to create some questions that speak clearly and directly to this particular person. I encourage you to experiment with these questions, to modify them for the person and situation as needed, and to create your own.

Whether or not the person has immediate answers to your questions, the next thing you might do is to suggest that the two of you sit in silence and listen to God. I like to say to parishioners, "I will be praying for you while you are listening for God's guidance." This approach keeps me from the danger of believing that it is my job to speak for God to the person. God can speak to her without my help! It is my job to encourage her to listen.

You can also ask parishioners what Bible verses, stories, or hymns provide answers for their concern. If you are a pastor, and you are brave, you might ask about what sermons have provided help in addressing the person's goal. You could also guide people in spiritual practices, such as prayer, meditation, listening, journaling, walking the labyrinth, and centering prayer. You might ask about what practices your congregants have found meaningful. If time allows, do a spiritual practice in the session. If you used a practice in step one to facilitate your congregant's connection with God, you might ask what she heard from God. If time is short, encourage parishioners to do the practices as part of their plan of action.

Wisdom from God should be congruent with and add to wisdom from the person's higher self. If these messages are contradictory, the person has confused other voices with the voice of God or the voice of the higher self. One of my spiritual directors used to tell me that at times I confused the voice of my own tyrannical conscience with the voice of the Holy Spirit. I learned to discern what was happening by looking for growth toward Christlike love in the guidance I was hearing. If it was absent, confused, or confusing, then I discerned that my tyrannical conscience was contaminating the voice of God. This type of confusion can happen for your parishioners as well. You might find it helpful to invite them to discern if the messages they are hearing are truly congruent with the love and grace of God.

◇◇

When Theological Language Is Not Appropriate

If your ministry is in a nonreligious setting, helping the person to listen to God becomes more complicated. You can simplify the process by asking the person how she understands God or divinity or a higher power and using whatever language the person prefers. When I worked as a hospital chaplain I found that often people who did not claim a religious background were comfortable using the word *God*. Sometimes people preferred the words *the Divine* or *the Universe* or *Spirit*. I have found that most people have been able to connect with *the Divine* or *Spirit*.

When I talk with people who do not want to seek help from God (using any language) I simply skip this part of step four. I seek to meet them where they are and to help with what they have requested of me. Seeking wisdom from their higher selves and from other people is sufficient. Sometimes doing so leads to deeper spiritual discussions later and sometimes it does not.

◇◇

Listen to Others

It is natural for you as a pastor to bring your experiences, skills, thoughts, instincts, and abilities into the conversation with your parishioner. Remember, though, that you are the person's minister, which means that you are responsible for guiding the search, not for its outcome. In other words, participate fully in the search for possibilities but do not take over. Your parishioner remains the expert. It is not your responsibility to "find the answer." That duty belongs to your congregant. Your responsibility is to guide the process.

If you find that you are focused on "finding the right answer for the person," "fixing her," or "solving her problem," you might consider that you are taking over the function that belongs to your parishioner. A pastoral supervisor once told me that the more intensity ministers feel about giving someone an answer, the more likely it is that they should wait and examine themselves and this impulse. Intensity is an indication that this response is about *you*, not about your parishioner. A spiritual guide once told me that the Holy Spirit does not use the word *should*, as in the phrase "You *should* do *this*." On the other hand, when an idea is inspired, the energy will feel warm and inviting rather than intense or desperate. It will feel like an invitation rather than a demand.

While your primary task is to guide the CARING process, you might consider yourself, the minister, as one of the people your parishioner can connect with for help. As you are brainstorming together, share your ideas with humility. Because people tend to give ministers excessive authority, I find it helpful to invite people to assess my ideas from their own wisdom when I offer possibilities. I often say something like, "You know more about your situation than I do. I offer my ideas as a possibility for you to consider, not as a way to tell you what to do. You might accept what I suggest, you might reject it, or you might modify it. I am involved in the search for solutions with you. I am not the expert telling you what to do." If I want to be less wordy, I might say matter-of-factly, "Does that idea work for you or is it off in some way?" This question invites the person to interact with and assess your ideas rather than uncritically accept them.

Numerous powerful questions can help the person access the wisdom of other people. You might ask, "Who do you know who does "x" well? Could you ask him to mentor you in learning how? If so, when will you contact him?" If the person does not want to be mentored, you might ask, "What have you observed that he does?" or "What do you think he does?" You could also ask your parishioner, "Who would be willing to help and support you?" and "What resources do you know about from other people's experiences—books, bibliographies, or blogs?" or "How can you research this topic, using resources from other people?" An additional powerful spiritual question is "Who are the people who love you and how have they offered to help? Are you willing to ask for and receive their help?" If your parishioner is willing to do so, this activity is added to the brainstorming list. If he is not willing, you might follow up with "Do you want us to look for a way around the block that is keeping you from being willing to ask for and receive help?" If he wants to work on the difficulty, you do so in the next step. If he says no, it is better to accept his judgment than to cajole him or try to change his mind. People often have good reasons for the changes they resist. Perhaps the timing or circumstance or setting is not right for that particular action.

Obviously, as you are inviting people to listen to God, their higher selves, and other people for inspiration, you will not ask every possible question I have listed. You will need to choose the ones that are most appropriate to the circumstance and the person's needs. The agreed-upon focus for the conversation is a reliable guide for which questions and practices are most appropriate to your congregant's needs. You might also choose questions that combine these categories, such as, "What actions would address your goal and be loving to yourself, other people, and God?"

Develop an Inspired Action Plan

Your work in guiding your parishioner thus far through this step has been about seeking and capturing inspired ideas for a loving action plan. Listening to her higher self, listening to God, and listening to wisdom from other people are the categories that will now contribute to an inspired action plan. The final aspect of step four is to develop this action plan. This process is easiest if you have kept a list of the possible actions as you were brainstorming with your congregant. If you have a list then review together all the ideas you have written down. Say something like, "Let's look over all of the possible actions we have listed and I would like to hear from you which action steps you are willing to commit to doing." You could also ask, "Considering this entire list, what seems like the best plan of action to you?" Alternatively, you might look at the list together and suggest that the parishioner determine which ideas she wants to include in her action plan.

If you have not kept a list, modify these questions as you and your parishioner construct an action plan from your memory of the conversation. You might ask something like, "Considering everything we have discussed, what items do you want to include in your action plan?" You could also say, "It is time now to create a plan of action from the possibilities we have discussed. What action steps are you willing to commit to taking?" In my experience, most of the time people are able to answer these questions with surprising ease and clarity.

When Developing an Action Plan Is Difficult

Sometimes, however, your parishioner will struggle to discover ideas for action. You may have guided your parishioner through a thorough search for possibilities and find that the answers are elusive or the person is not clear about what he wants to do. Several options exist to assist your parishioner in developing an action plan in this circumstance. First, you might slow the conversation down and again invite the search for wisdom. You could say, "Let us stop and be silent for a moment to listen for guidance from God and our own higher wisdom" or "Would you like to pray and listen for God's guidance right now?" Clarity can emerge from slowing down, being still, and listening for guidance.

Second, sometimes people need to do some research, to gather information, before they are ready to develop a plan to address their goal. In a similar manner, sometimes people need a time of prayer, contemplation, and discernment before they are ready to create an action plan. In these cases, doing research or spending time in prayer *is* the next step to help the person move toward where he wants to be. Research or prayer becomes the action plan. You are meeting the person where he is. You do not have to map out the entire route from where he is to where he wants to be. Sometimes discovering the next step is enough, like driving down a dark road at night. You can only see as far as your headlights illuminate and you have to continue traveling to see farther. Searching for an action, a first step, even a baby step in the right direction helps people plan movement and develop some momentum, which in turn can help them see and travel farther down their path.

Encouraging people to experiment can also be helpful when developing an action plan is difficult. Experiments help people to learn from their experience whether or not they solve the problem. Experiments help people make progress in many ways, such as by discovering part of the answer, something that does not work, or something that does help. Parishioners might increase their knowledge or experience in a way that clarifies the next step. If creating an action plan is difficult, consider if an experiment is needed.

When you find yourself stuck at any point in the CARING conversation, it could be because one of the previous steps needs to be revisited to give you more information about the problem and possible solutions. It is possible that you have wandered away from the goal of the conversation. Simply restating the realistic focus you developed in step three can do wonders to sharpen and clarify a pastoral conversation.

The most likely scenario if you are feeling stuck at this point is that the focus for the conversation was unclear or too big. If so, revisit the focus of the conversation you agreed upon in step three. Restate it and say, "Perhaps we are stuck because this goal is too big. What is a smaller piece of this goal that we can work with now? It needs to be small enough to allow us to plan some actions that could be done in the next week." It is also possible that the goal itself is the problem. Is it truly congruent with the individual's faith and spirituality? Is it truly what the person wants to get from this conversation with you? This additional focusing and narrowing and assessing the goal often generate movement when conversations are stalled at this point.

Sometimes, when you are stuck in a CARING conversation with a parishioner, something important has not been discussed. For example, you do not have time in step two to hear everything important about where she is, what the difficulties are, and where she wants to be. Sometimes significant material is left out. You might address this fact with questions to your congregant. You might say, "What should I ask you that I'm not asking?" or "What do I not know that I need to know to help?" These powerful questions can restart a stalled pastoral conversation.

Perhaps there is a difficulty that is preventing the person from finding possible solutions. In this case, discovering and removing the block is the next phase of the person's journey. You might ask your congregant, "What is your biggest block regarding (restate the goal of the conversation)?" If the person is able to name a difficulty, then the action plan becomes finding ways around the block. If the person is not able to name a struggle, then the action plan becomes recognizing the blocks to the goal (and then finding a way around them). Suggest the appropriate action plan and ask for the person's agreement. If she has objections, that information can help you develop a plan that will work, or they might indicate a need for referral.

Being unable to guide your parishioner to a plan could be a sign that you need to consider referring the person to someone else for help. You will need to consider whether she needs pastoral guidance or therapeutic help. If you determine that your parishioner needs therapeutic help, then follow the guidelines in chapter 2 and other pastoral care resources and refer her for therapy. Sometimes your judgment might be that the person's need is for spiritual care or pastoral conversations, but for some reason your guidance is not helping her. At this point, you have two options. One is to request consultation or supervision from a specialist in pastoral care. You might already have a consultant or supervisor you can ask for help. If not, some certified members of the Association for Clinical Pastoral Education offer consultation for ministers. A pastoral care specialist can help you determine what issues are getting in the way of your pastoral conversations and what to do differently. Your second option is to refer the person to another minister for pastoral care and conversation.

Assess the Plan

After the action plan has been developed, then you can guide your parishioner to assess the plan. You might ask, "Is it loving?" "Is it wise?" and "Is it mature?" You might also ask, "Is it congruent with your spirituality and moral commitments?" Other questions for assessing the plan are "Will this action plan help you meet your goal for the conversation?" and "Will this plan help you move to where you want to be?" If any of these questions indicate ways that the plan should be changed, ask the person to modify it. Then ask the person to state his plan or to write it down. You want to be sure that you clearly understand the action plan the person has made because in the next step you will be helping him address any obstacles he has to working his plan.

Pitfalls to Avoid

Several pitfalls should be avoided as you guide the person through this step. The primary one is the temptation to believe that making the plan and coming up with actions is your responsibility. In the CARING process, it is not. It is your responsibility to ask powerful questions and to facilitate the person's connection with her resources. It is the person's responsibility to come up with possible actions, to evaluate them, and to decide which ones to commit to take.

Not writing things down might lead to a pitfall. It is easy to lose track of all the good ideas that will emerge during step four. Trusting your memory may mean that important material is overlooked in the creation of the plan.

Accepting the initial idea as the plan without exploring other sources of wisdom could also be a pitfall. This shortcut might mean that you do not reach inspired action, but stop with what comes to mind first. Go through the entire step. On the other hand, if there is a clear "aha" that you and the person both feel inspired by, it might be a pitfall to follow all of the guidelines pedantically. There is a time to say "That's it!" and move on to the next steps of the process. Learning to recognize inspired action will come with experience and practice.

It is a pitfall to spend so much time on this step that you shortchange the next two phases of the CARING process. Be aware of your time constraints so that time is allotted for the next two steps. You might have to choose one powerful question for each of the three sources of knowledge if the conversation is a brief one. In a very brief conversation, you might use one powerful question that incorporates all three, such as, "Making use of all the wisdom available to you from your higher self, God, and other people's experiences, what loving actions might help you meet your goal?" If it is a longer conversation, you have more time to delve into this topic and ask more powerful questions, but you will need to stay aware of the time.

Integrating Previous Steps and Ongoing Use of This Step

The fourth step will naturally align with the first step because your parishioner will need to connect with God, her higher self, and other people in order to seek their wisdom to address her concerns. You will want to listen to your own higher self and to God throughout the search for a loving, inspired action plan. Attending to the journey will be an ongoing process, particularly because this step focuses on possible ways for the person to move from where she is to where she wants to be. As the person explores this question, obstacles may arise and you will make note of them so that you will be prepared to address the obstacles in the next step.

The agreed-upon focus is used to keep the brainstorming in this step on track. You may need to remind the person (and yourself!) of the focus of the conversation, perhaps several times. You integrate the careful work of the third step into step four when you use the exact words of the agreed-upon goal of the conversation as you are exploring. You do this with questions like these: "How might God help you meet *this goal* (restate it)?" and "What possible actions would your higher self suggest to meet *this goal* (restate it)?" and "Who else do you know who might help you with *this goal* (restate it)?" and "What loving actions could you take to meet *this goal* (restate it)?" All three previous steps are integrated into this fourth step of inviting help, brainstorming, and creating an action plan.

As you move forward you will want to stay alert for additional inspired actions that emerge as the conversation continues. You might also watch for times in which it is appropriate to ask for

God's help, or to ask the person to access his own higher wisdom. In addition, there may be times to offer your own responses or suggestions or to ask the person about how other people might assist him.

How to Know You Have Completed This Step

You will know that you have completed this step when you have taken the following actions.

- You have heard and written down or remembered the person's spontaneous ideas.

- You have asked the person what other ideas she has.

- You have contributed your own ideas and invited the person to assess them.

- You have not given answers or advice that you feel desperate about providing.

- You have invited the person to access wisdom from God.

- You have invited the person to access her higher self.

- You have invited the person to access help from other people.

- You have noted the actions called for by the "aha" moments.

- You may have a feeling of completion or satisfaction.

- You may notice that your parishioner expresses satisfaction, relief, or joy.

- You have guided the person to create an action plan.

- You have assessed if the plan is loving, and modified it if needed.

Once you have guided your parishioner to an action plan, it is time to move to the next step in the process. When the congregant has chosen a solution to her problem that she would like to explore, it is time to consider the obstacles that might hinder this path and to make a plan to navigate around them. This topic will be discussed in the next chapter.

Chapter Five

STEP 5: NAVIGATE AROUND OBSTACLES

This chapter will teach you how to help your parishioner notice, release, and navigate around obstacles that hinder the success of his plan. In this step you will choose an important obstacle to help him navigate around. The obstacle you choose to work with should be an obstacle to the plan he has just created to help him reach the goal. In this step, you want to help the person name the obstacles that might be getting in his way. You also want to help him find ways to manage these obstacles most effectively. Sometimes that means releasing them. Sometimes it means navigating around them. Sometimes it means making changes so that the obstacle is less likely to occur. In all instances, the purpose of this step is to know what might hinder him in accomplishing his plan and to be prepared to address those obstacles in ways that lead to success.

If you have been in ministry for any length of time or have paid attention to your own life experience, you know that many times human beings make plans and do not follow through with them. Romans 7:15 describes this aspect of human life perfectly: "I don't know what I'm doing, because I don't do what I want to do. Instead, I do the thing that I hate." Step five is designed to address this aspect of human experience. As you help people recognize and navigate around their obstacles, you are making it more likely that they will achieve their goals for the conversations.

Throughout life people create beliefs about themselves, other people, God, and how the world works. Sometimes the concepts that people believe to be true are actually false beliefs or hindrances to their lives. Persons often take action based on their false beliefs. For example, a person who believes, deep down, "If I am successful at my job, then I will lose the love and support of my family and friends" has (what appears to be) a good reason to sabotage her plans for succeeding at her job. Parishioners may need help to remember that there are good purposes behind their resistance to goals they want to achieve. The term "resistance movement" illustrates this concept. Something negative, problematic, wrong, difficult, or evil is being resisted. Sometimes discovering the good purpose will help people release their resistance when it is based on a belief that is not true. Problems occur when people act on false beliefs. Discovering and helping people change false beliefs help them to succeed with their loving action plan.

Removing obstacles will free the person to take action. Imagine a person is trying to drive a car with one foot on the accelerator and the other foot on the brake. A lot of energy is being expended. One part of the system is fighting against another part. This conflict may lead to some damage. The journey is impeded as the driver is not traveling very far or very fast. It is an experience of being stuck. Removing obstacles might be like helping the person to take her foot off the brake. She will get unstuck and begin to move forward. She will also need to be prepared to steer in the direction she wants to go. In other situations, removing obstacles can be like helping the person take her foot off the accelerator and make a clear commitment to brake. Sometimes, the right decision is to stop. In traveling on a journey sometimes you need to accelerate and sometimes you need to brake, but you do not need to do both at the same time. Trying to do both at the same time, generally, means either that there is something about your situation that you need to understand more fully, or there is a decision or commitment that you need to make, or both.

Introduce and Begin This Step

Use whatever concepts resonate for you from the above discussion to introduce this step to your congregant. You could also say something like, "Of course, knowing what to do is not the main thing when it comes to success. Actually doing it is the key. In many parts of life, we know exactly what to do but find difficulty actually doing what we know. I hope to increase your chances of success by exploring and removing obstacles to the action plan we have developed." The CARING process does not require that you explain each step. You could skip the explanation if it feels contrived or unnecessary to you. Simply go straight to the conversational guidance I offer next.

A Conversational Process

The easiest way to begin this step is conversationally. You would begin with a question designed to identify and name any obstacles to the person's ability to follow the action plan that was formed in step four. You might ask a question like one of these: "What would get in your way?" "What might keep you from doing what you've planned?" and "How might you sabotage yourself?" I often ask all three questions, but if I only have time for one question, I ask some version of "How might you sabotage yourself?" With a young person, I might say, "If you were going to mess this up, what would you do? How would you mess it up?" With someone who has been trying to solve the problem for a period of time, I might say, "You have been trying things. You know yourself well. What would you be likely to do that would sabotage your progress?"

You can address obstacles by asking the person, "Do you feel uneasy about any part of your plan?" and "Is there any aspect of it you might avoid?" You will be amazed at how easily most people know the answers to these questions. People will sometimes laugh at themselves, or be rueful, but they do tend to answer honestly. If you feel that it would be helpful for you and your parishioner for him to share in more depth and specificity, you can ask, "Tell me more about that" or "What does that look like?" Sometimes the person names one obstacle in response to this question and at other times he might name more than one.

When There Are Several Obstacles

When the person has named several obstacles, it is helpful to address the most significant one in the pastoral conversation. If you have time, you can deal with the lesser obstacles, but you want to discern the most important one to tackle. A helpful approach when the problem is complicated, there are multiple obstacles, your time is limited, or any combination of these, would be to say, "At this stage of the conversation, I want to help you remove the biggest obstacle to reaching your goal. What would you say that is?" You can also say something like, "As I have been listening to you share about changing your situation, these are the obstacles I have heard you mention. (List them.) Which obstacle would you like my help in removing today?"

At this point you can invite the person to listen to God and her higher self for guidance. You might pray together as you decide which obstacle to address. Sometimes the biggest one will make sense as a place to start. At other times, there might be one obstacle that logically needs to be addressed first. Another good choice is an obstacle that the person feels stuck about or has not found a way to address on her own. When you have completed the first four steps, it often becomes clear which obstacle needs immediate focus in step five. A good guideline is to address whatever obstacle might get in the way of reaching the goal or completing the action steps.

You do not have to be perfectionistic about this step of identifying an obstacle. In fact, perfectionism can get in the way of your higher, more creative and wise self. Make your best choice and keep moving through the process. If you have missed something important, the person will become aware of it. I believe that one of the graces of ministry is that when ministers overlook something important, parishioners will usually mention the issue again. If we continue paying attention, we will notice the person's repeated concern. The topic will circle back around.

In fact, if you do become perfectionistic at this stage, it can be a sign that you have confused your role in the process. It is the person's job to identify their obstacle(s) to share with you. It is *your* job to ask the person what obstacle he would choose to overcome, and to offer guidance as he makes a plan to do so. Simply ask your congregant to focus on an obstacle that is significantly hampering the ability to take action to meet the goal of the conversation. Overcoming even one obstacle will help the person make progress. The combination of being heard, deciding on a starting point, developing an inspired action plan, and overcoming obstacles is powerful and often propels the person forward toward where he wants to be.

Once the obstacle has been identified, it is time to help the person get around it or through it. We have discussed earlier in this chapter a direct conversational approach. You might choose to simply follow that process. If you have additional time, and you sense that the person needs in-depth help with his obstacles, I recommend the following processes.

Getting around an Obstacle

Questions to help a person navigate around an obstacle might include "How might you avoid doing this or that?" "How would you know if you are inadvertently beginning to sabotage your goal?" "What could you do instead?" and "How might you get around that obstacle?" People often come up with very useful and creative ideas on the spot, as they process the dilemma aloud with you in conversation.

If the obstacle is another person's behavior, you will want to use great care in how you address the issue. You do not want to take the position that you and your parishioner are going to figure out how to change the other person's behavior. That is an impossible goal! You cannot directly influence someone who is not in the room. It *is* possible to work with your parishioner about how he will *respond* to the obstacle the other person is putting in the way.

For example, suppose you are working with a woman who wants to lose weight. One of the obstacles she names is that her husband brings her treats and encourages her to enjoy them. He is unhappy when she does not indulge in the treats he brings her and says things like, "I just want you to have something good." You might ask, "How does this affect you?" to explore the rest of her situation. That he brings her treats is part of the obstacle. Her choice to eat food she does not want to prevent his sad feelings is another part of the obstacle. You can explore this type of situation by asking, "Are there internal obstacles that his behavior is eliciting in you?" You might also say, "Let's deal with the aspects of this problem that you can control."

When other people are presented as the obstacle, there are several powerful questions you can ask. To continue with the example, you might ask this woman, "How can you enlist him to be on your side?" and "How can you explain what you are doing so that the people close to you will support your efforts rather than sabotage them?" and "If this is not possible, how can you deal with the saboteurs in a way that holds on to your goals while not damaging (or perhaps even improving) the relationship?" Finally, you might ask, "What do you need to change about your own thoughts, feelings, and actions to make these more loving behaviors possible?" or "Who do you need to be to make these changes?" These powerful questions are useful for many situations in which another person is presented as the obstacle.

More In-Depth Help

Sometimes the process already outlined in this chapter will be enough to help the individual name and plan a way to work around the obstacles. At other times, the person might need more specific help from you. When deeper attention is needed, Brooke Castillo's model can be very helpful to use in your pastoral conversation.

You will remember that Castillo's model is that "Circumstances create Thoughts, which create Feelings, which create Actions, which create Results."[1] The implication for helping people change is obvious. People can change their results by changing their actions, and people can change their actions by changing their feelings, and people can change their feelings by changing their thoughts.

When the Obstacle Is a Thought

Sometimes people can recognize the thoughts that are obstacles simply by being asked the question "What thoughts do you have that are creating a block to getting what you want?" or "What thoughts will block you from following through with the action plan we just agreed upon?" At other times people need additional help.

Castillo recommends helping people to find the thoughts that need to be changed by guiding people to work through her model of change. In her book *Self Coaching 101*, she gives the following example of a model a client filled out based on a particular problem.

- CIRCUMSTANCE: She did not show up on time.

- THOUGHT: She does not respect me.

- FEELING: Angry, sad, rejected.

- ACTION: Act passive-aggressive. Make snide comments.

- RESULT: Less respect from her.[2]

The client then sought a different thought that would cause different feelings, actions, and results. The circumstance is the same, but everything else is different in response to the new thought.

- CIRCUMSTANCE: She did not show up on time.
- THOUGHT: She must be busy—I won't take it personally.
- FEELING: Appreciative she made it, relaxed.
- ACTION: Act with kindness and understanding.
- RESULT: No effect personally—no negativity.[3]

You can help a person use this model by putting the problem he has named in the appropriate line in the model and then helping him to see the connections and fill out the rest of the model. For example, if the problem a person names is an action (or lack of action) you can ask, "What feelings are leading to that action?" When he has named a feeling, you can ask, "What thoughts are leading to that feeling?" When you have heard the thought, Castillo recommends asking the person to change it for a better thought and filling out a new model that will lead to the result he wants.[4]

Once the thought has been recognized, I recommend a modification to her process. I find it helpful to assess whether the thought is true or not before taking the step of changing the thought. If the thought is a false belief, as discussed above, then changing it is the appropriate next step, and I suggest that ministers guide people to choose more loving and true thoughts to replace unloving and false ones. However, if the thought *is* true, it must be addressed as an accurate reflection of the situation. The true thought might give you clues about how to better address the real situation by modifying the action plan.

As an example, let us consider Castillo's illustration about the person who had the thought "She does not respect me."[5] In some instances that thought would be false and changing it, as Castillo suggests, would be appropriate. In other instances, the thought might be true, therefore giving the person needed information. If the thought "she is disrespecting me" is true, then it provides information that something needs to be changed in the relationship or something needs attention. Obviously, we cannot know with certainty the truth of someone else's thoughts or attitudes. A more verifiable thought would be "I interpret her behavior as disrespectful. I believe there is something wrong between us." Recognizing and acknowledging a truth often gives people information about needed changes.

The person with the problem would be better served by addressing the issues in the relationship than by changing his thoughts, in this case. If the thought is true, you guide your parishioner to learn what he needs to learn from it and to adjust his action plan accordingly. If the thought is false, you guide your parishioner to choose a different thought.

When the Obstacle Is a Feeling

If your parishioner has feelings that are obstacles to her plan of action, then the pastoral questions (previously discussed in chapter 4) can be asked. Remember that these questions are designed to help people use their emotions constructively rather than destructively. The goal of the pastoral questions is to help persons choose appropriate and loving actions in response to feelings. If the obstacle is anger you might ask the pastoral questions for anger: "What is the threat?"[6] "What must be protected?" and "What must be restored?"[7] Additionally, you can understand anger as serving the function of correcting injustice and can ask the questions "How can I overcome injustice?" "How might I change myself?" and "How might I change my situation?"[8] If the obstacle is sadness, you could ask the pastoral questions for sadness: "What needs to be released?" and "What needs to be renewed or rejuvenated?"[9] You might also ask, "What needs to be grieved?" adding that Jesus said that those who grieve will be made glad (Matt 5:4). If the obstacle is fear, then you ask the pastoral questions for fear: "Do you need to run from danger, or do you need to face your fear?" or "What are you wanting to protect?"[10] Recognizing that fear calls us into action, you can also ask, "What action must you take?"[11] or "What do you need to do to be prepared for the situation you fear that you might encounter?"[12]

Because fear is often underneath feelings of sadness and anger, having spiritual resources for dealing with fear is particularly important. If fear is getting in the person's way, then prayer and other spiritual resources can be used to help the person choose love and release fear. At this point you might introduce one or more biblical passages to guide persons who are experiencing fear. You can choose one or more that seems to speak to the person's specific situation.

A passage I find to be particularly helpful is Philippians 4:6-7:

> Don't be anxious about anything; rather, bring up all of your requests to God in your prayers and petitions, along with giving thanks. Then the peace of God that exceeds all understanding will keep your hearts and minds safe in Christ Jesus.

These verses guide people through a prayer process that helps them to release their anxiety and experience God's peace.

This passage begins by exhorting people "Don't be anxious" and inviting them to pray. I think of the meaning of verse 6 as this: whenever you are worried or anxious then you should pray. We can begin to see our fears as an invitation to turn to God in prayer. Doing so is one way that we can prepare for situations we fear. We are also instructed to offer prayer, petitions (earnest emotional requesting), and thanksgiving to God (v. 6). We are invited to bring our requests to God (v. 6). I find this language helpful. I am invited to bring up all of my requests to God with an attitude of prayer, emotional earnestness, and gratitude. This language invites me to be both serious and childlike in the requests I make of God. I am careful and thoughtful about the requests I bring up to God. The passage suggests that this process brings us to the experience of the peace of God, but it doesn't stop with the promise of the experience of divine peace; it goes on to say that the peace of God will keep our hearts and minds safe in Christ Jesus (v. 7). Turning away from anxiety and turning toward prayer, authenticity, and gratitude—bringing our requests to God—will then result in the peace of God keeping our hearts and minds safe in Christ Jesus.[13] Choosing faith and trust in God propels the journey from anxiety to peace.

This passage describes a prayer journey of moving from anxiety to having our thoughts and feelings reside in Christ Jesus. You can teach about this passage or quote it as you invite your parishioners to bring their fears to God in search of peacefully abiding in Christ. You can use this material either to guide people to pray about their fears with you in the session or on their own as they notice their feelings of fear blocking their actions, or both. One of the best actions people can take in response to fear is to pray.

In some circumstances when the obstacle is a feeling, you might not want to use the pastoral questions. Your time might be limited. The problem might be close to one that is happening in your own life and you rightly feel that you are not in a good place to explore the feelings deeply with the parishioner. In this instance, you will need to decide if you need to refer the individual to someone else, or if you could use Castillo's model of asking about the thought that led to the feelings and guiding the person to change the thought as described above. Of course, when there is an important emotional issue in your own life, you would be wise to seek help.

You might not have the skills to address feelings with parishioners by using the pastoral questions. If this is the case, I encourage you to do some form of continuing education to improve your emotional intelligence. Clinical Pastoral Education in programs accredited by the ACPE is one way to do so. Contracting for supervision or consultation with a pastoral educator or pastoral counselor is another. I offer a course, "Emotional Intelligence for Ministry and Leadership," at Mercer University School of Theology.

When the Obstacle Is an Action or Inaction

When the obstacle is an action or inaction, you might ask the person to choose actions based on truth and love. You could also follow Castillo's model, asking what feelings have led to the person's behavior. Then you can either address the feelings using the pastoral questions or ask what thoughts led to the feelings. If you do the latter, then you can work with the thoughts as described above. If you do the former, the answers to the pastoral questions about feelings should guide the person to choose loving and helpful actions. Of course, you might address the obstacle by paying attention to both thoughts and feelings.

Getting around obstacles often includes helping people motivate themselves and manage their behavior. I have found one of Martha Beck's techniques particularly helpful for helping people overcome, release, or navigate around obstacles. For long and involved projects that feel overwhelming, Beck recommends a technique she calls turtle steps.[14] She considers turtle steps to be small and doable steps taken regularly, consistently, and slowly. A turtle step is a small step that feels easy to the person. It is the largest step that still feels like you could do it easily with no problem. She was inspired to create the technique by watching an occupational therapist work with her young son who has Down syndrome.[15]

Beck credits turtle steps with helping her write her dissertation. She had written nothing for months, while expecting herself to write for eight hours a day. When she created the technique, she mentally considered a commitment to write for six hours a day to be easy. But her body feelings were a definite no. She cut the time in half to try to find a turtle step—to write for three hours a day. Three hours still felt too long and intimidating for her. She cut it in half again, and ninety minutes a day did not feel easy. One hour felt difficult, as did thirty minutes of writing. Fifteen minutes a day felt completely easy and doable.

She made a commitment to write for fifteen minutes a day as a turtle step. She started writing fifteen minutes a day. Her rule for taking turtle steps is this: "You are not allowed to take another turtle step until twenty-four hours have passed or you feel a strong desire to move on, whichever comes first. At that point take one more turtle step. Then stop again and so on."[16] Some days she stopped after fifteen minutes, having successfully met her goal, and waited until the following day to write again. Other days she wrote paragraphs or pages. Following this process she wrote her dissertation in a year.[17] That is how she completed her PhD at Harvard!

I have used this process and have shared it with my students. It seems to work for a variety of projects and personalities. I encourage you to try it and, when it seems appropriate, to share it with your parishioners.

Whatever obstacle you choose to address, step five is about helping your parishioner navigate around the obstacles to the action plan that was created in step four. I have found that people are generally able to talk about how they might sabotage their plans. I have also found that people can easily come up with strategies to avoid self-sabotage and to get around their obstacles. You will improve your congregant's chances of success if you ask him to notice and navigate around his obstacles to reaching his goal.

Pitfalls to Avoid

Some pastors might be tempted to skip this step. It seems logical to move from making the plan to making the commitment to the plan in all its specifics. But if there are obstacles, they need to be addressed because removing the obstacles creates the opportunity for the person to succeed. It is important not to skip this step. It empowers the person to make a change in an area with which she has been struggling. Navigating around obstacles makes change more likely and easier.

Also, avoid the pitfall of trying to deal with every obstacle that has been named throughout the conversation. You have to discriminate and invite the person to choose the most important one because you do not have unlimited time. Even if you did have unlimited time, trying to address every obstacle would likely overwhelm the person and backfire. So, choose the most important and do not try to do everything.

Again, avoid the pitfall of believing that it is your job to give the person answers. It is your job to guide the conversation and to ask powerful questions. It is your parishioner's job to seek help and wisdom and answers. It is your parishioners job to determine how to navigate around her obstacles.

Integrating Previous Steps and Ongoing Use of This Step

All four previous steps are useful as you help the person to notice obstacles and find a way to navigate around them. Dealing with obstacles can be intimidating or frightening, so maintaining and facilitating the person's connections with God, his higher self, you, and other people is important as you guide him through this process.

In choosing which obstacle to deal with, you will want to be attuned to where your congregant wants to be (step two), the goal he has chosen for this conversation (step three), and the plan he has made (step four). You will want to continue attending to his journey as you talk with him about the obstacles to the plan that he is seeking to overcome. You will want to continue keeping the conversation focused on the goal you have agreed upon as you work on navigating around the obstacles. And, of course, you will want to stay aware of the plan your congregant has made as he discusses finding a way around the obstacles to achieving this plan.

Of course, as you advance to step six, Generate Commitment to a Specific, Loving Action Plan, you will want to continue noticing and navigating around obstacles. Asking for a specific commitment might cause resistance to emerge, and you are now equipped to guide your parishioner to address it. The CARING process flows logically, and the steps enhance each other.

How to Know You Have Completed This Step

You have completed this step when you have accomplished the following activities.

- You have asked the person what obstacles might prevent her from following her plan. (You have asked questions like, "How might you unintentionally sabotage this plan?" "Do you feel uneasy about any aspect of the process?" and "Is there any part of this plan that you might avoid?")

- You have a clear understanding of the most important obstacle preventing the person from achieving her goal.

- Your conversational work has helped to remove perceived obstacles and you have brainstormed together ways the person can overcome obstacles.

- You have addressed thoughts, feelings, actions, or all of these, that may function in and of themselves as an obstacle.

- You have adjusted the plan when needed to enable the person to navigate around her obstacles or unexpected obstacles.

Having completed this work, you will advance to step six of the CARING process.

Chapter Six

STEP 6: GENERATE COMMITMENT TO A SPECIFIC, LOVING ACTION PLAN

You are ready now to move to the final step of the CARING process. You have helped the person connect with God, himself, and others. You have attended to his journey from where he is to where he wants to be and have heard the difficulties he has encountered. You have assessed that a CARING pastoral conversation is appropriate for his particular concern. You have reached agreement with him about the area of focus and the goal for this particular conversation. You have invited him to seek guidance from God, his higher self, and other people, and to develop action steps to address his goal. You have helped him to notice and navigate around his obstacles to taking these steps. It is time now to generate specifics of the plan and his commitments to them.

Conversations that inspire change should end with agreement on an action plan. The agreement will describe specific action steps the person plans to make. The most effective action plans will include commitments to the time and place the steps will be taken. Asking for a commitment to the plan also helps people to follow through with their action plans. Lastly, schedule a time for a follow-up session or report to assess the person's progress and make adjustments as needed.

Generate Commitment to a Specific Plan of Action

As you begin the process of generating a specific plan of action, it is important to be clear about the differences between your responsibilities and your parishioner's responsibilities. It is your parishioner's job to generate the plan, and it is your job to facilitate this process. You ask powerful questions, reflect what you hear, and help the person clarify her plan. She comes up with the action steps she wants to take; she makes the commitment to action.

You invite her to be accountable to herself, not to you. It is not your job to "make" her do the work she has outlined. You can invite her to think about people and activities that can help her be successful. You do not have to "hold her accountable." You do invite her to be accountable to herself, not to you. You can ask her to follow up with you as a way to invite her to be accountable to herself. She is responsible for her actions or inactions. She will reap the benefits or consequences of her behavior.

A simple conversational way to begin this process is to ask the question "From everything we have talked about and everything you know about your situation, what are you willing to commit to do?" This is an effective question for several reasons. It invites him to draw from the whole conversation so that his commitments might be bigger or more integrated than simply using the action plan of step four. Drawing from the whole conversation also invites him to take into account navigating around the obstacles.

It is a powerful question because it invites him to go beyond this one conversation to draw upon wisdom from everything he knows. There may be important concepts he knows but has not discussed with you for any number of reasons, such as time constraints, embarrassment, or focusing on other things. This question invites him to access all of his wisdom and knowledge.

Asking for commitment is the third reason this question is so powerful. The plan now becomes something she is committed to do, not something she thinks she should do, or she thinks is right, or she believes her mother wants her to do, or she thinks you want her to do. It moves into the realm of reality. The question is genius because it ends with a call to action: "to do." It asks the person to survey the conversation and everything she knows to come up with actions that she is willing to commit to take.

I discovered the power of this question shortly after I had completed coach training. I was coaching a congregant. I got caught up in attending to the problem. I was interested, fascinated, and curious. I completely forgot about exploring where she wanted to go, much less the rest of the process or coming up with an action plan. I had talked with her for about forty-five minutes, exploring her problem in detail, when I suddenly realized that we had about five to ten minutes before the conversation would have to end and I had not done any of the coaching process. Chagrined and embarrassed, but also inspired, I jumped right to the end goal of a coaching conversation: developing a plan of action. I made up this question on the spot because I knew I had not covered everything. I asked, "From everything we have talked about and everything you know about your situation, what are you willing to commit to do?"

My congregant did a great job coming up with an inspired action plan that was perfect for her. I was once again reminded of the wisdom people have within them that can be accessed even when ministers do an imperfect job of guiding the process. I was also reminded that following my own wisdom and inspiration is a key to powerful problem-solving conversations. This question worked so well, I have been using it ever since, and now I am passing it on to you. As Dumbledore said to Harry in the first of the books about the boy wizard (Harry) and the old wise man (Dumbledore) who offers him much wisdom and guidance, "Use it well."[1] Like an invisibility cloak, this question allows your congregant to access information that she might not otherwise have accessible.

You can follow up on this question by asking, "What else?" a time or two until you feel that the person has expressed the plan he is willing to make a commitment to do. Once you have an action plan in place, it is time to turn the conversation to the specifics of the plan. It is crucial that the steps in the action plan are clear, specific, measurable, and scheduled.

The Importance of Specifics

I have found that the more specific people are in their planning, the more likely they seem to be in following through on their goals. Making decisions about specifics are like mustard seeds (Matt 13:31) and yeast (Matt 13:33). These choices are small things that lead to big changes. Clarifying specifics can be done by asking powerful questions like these: "When will you do the action?" "Where will you do it?" "How will you accomplish the behavior?" and "Who will help and support you?" I recommend that you use all of these questions and more as you lead people through the final step of the CARING process. Helping people be specific will greatly improve their chances of success in carrying out their plan.

Once your parishioner has named his plan, then you talk with him about specifics. You might say something like, "You've told me what you're willing to commit to do. Now let's improve your chances to be successful by planning ahead for the specifics of your actions." Then, ask a series of specific questions allowing him to respond to each one. It helps to capture the answers to these questions in writing. You might say, "We've talked about what you are going to do. Now let's talk about how you are going to do it. What ideas do you have?" A good follow-up question is this: "When will you do the steps of your plan?" It is very helpful to write these answers down. Next, ask, "Where will you do the steps of your plan?" Again, write the answers down.

You might also ask, "Who can help you?" and "When and where will you discuss this issue with the people who might help?" Organizations or agencies might be available to support your parishioner in accomplishing his goals. You can ask the person what resources might be available to him. If you know of additional resources, it would be appropriate to recommend some options for your parishioner to consider.

I have suggested writing down when and where. It can be quite helpful to have your parishioner actually put the steps and details on her calendar. Doing so is the first step of following through on the action plan. It will help to crystallize her commitment. It will also help her to see any issues related to place and time.

I often demonstrate the CARING process by helping people with common goals like exercising regularly. On one such occasion, a "parishioner" had tried to start an exercise plan without any success for quite a while. I took him through the CARING process and the action plan he decided upon was to exercise at the gym in the mornings, shower there, and then go to work. He had followed this plan successfully in the past and was quite excited about doing so again.

I asked him to write the commitment to exercise in his calendar, so that he would be clear about the times and days that he planned to go to the gym. He picked up his calendar with optimism and hope, excited about starting his new routine. As he looked at his week his face fell. He turned the page and looked at another week and shook his head in dismay. He turned several pages and looked upset. I asked him what he had seen. He said, "There is not a single morning in the next month that isn't already scheduled. I have a lot of breakfast meetings and some committee meetings. I have to leave early to drive to some things."

Because I asked him to write down when and where in his calendar, we uncovered an obstacle to this particular plan. In order for him to be successful, we then needed to circle back to step five and deal with this particular obstacle. He needed to change the when and where of his plan to exercise, reschedule some morning meetings, or both. He did not feel good about rescheduling commitments he had already made, but he did want to begin the habit of exercising first thing in the day as he had remembered how much it had helped him in the past.

He decided to do two things. First, he went through his calendar and scheduled exercise where he could. Some days that was at the end of the day. Some days when he had morning meetings and evening activities but a lighter schedule around noon, he scheduled exercise then. Second, he turned to the part of his calendar that was clear because he had not scheduled activities yet. He calendared his exercise as he wanted to do it in the mornings at the gym, with the idea that he would schedule other activities around his commitment to exercise.

I find that asking people to put things on the calendar often uncovers issues that need to be addressed in order for them to be successful. Scheduling commitments addresses the questions of who will do what, when, and where. Does that sound familiar to you? It is the old outline for a newspaper article. When I was in grammar school I was taught an outline for a newspaper story. Five words beginning with *W* form the structure: who, what, when, where, and why. So far in my discussion of the process we have covered all of these except the final one, why.

I find it important to say to congregants, "Let's remember why you are making this commitment. What is the important reason for your plan?" near the end of the discussion in step six. This reminds them of what they hope to achieve and the significance of their goal. Motivation is enhanced for following their action plan when they remember why it is important to them.

If it is appropriate to the person's worldview, you can ask about the spiritual significance of her plan. Especially if you have talked about the spiritual aspects of the problem and goal, this could be a good time to ask if the plan will help her become more loving, or move toward Christlike love, or grow spiritually. Confirming that the actions chosen are loving to self, others, and God is an important aspect of considering the *why* of the person's commitments.

Review the Action Plan

After you have asked about specifics, it is helpful to review the action plan with your congregant. If you have not done so earlier, this can be a helpful time to write the plan down, including the specifics. To begin this part of the conversation, you might say, "Are you willing to commit to doing the plan as we have just discussed?" or, even better, "Would you state your commitment or intentions out loud?" or "Let's recap. What are you going to do? When and where? Who will help you? Why are you making these commitments?" As you are generating commitment, there is one vital point for you to remember and to reinforce with your parishioner. The commitment is to herself and her plan; it is not to you.

You can also review the action plan with your parishioner to make sure the action plan is loving, advances love, and is motivated by love. Simply asking these questions of your parishioner will invite her to be certain her plan is loving and to modify it if needed. Help her to choose actions that are loving for herself, God, and other people.

As you are reviewing the plan, you can also ask if the plan meets the goal you set for the conversation. If it does, remark upon how well the person has achieved his goal. If it does not, then you may want to invite the parishioner to add some steps, or modify his plan in some way to meet the goal you set for this conversation.

Support and Encourage

You can support the actions your congregant chooses to take by offering encouragement and supporting her strengths. It is important at this stage of the process to offer sincere and whole-hearted encouragement to the person. Having walked with her through the process, your encouragement should feel natural. It should grow from your relationship with the person. In one class when I was demonstrating the CARING process for a group of MDiv students, the class was amazed at the change in body language they saw in the "parishioner" after I offered a few sentences of heartfelt encouragement. The students noticed that the person I was coaching sat up straighter, smiled, looked more powerful, and had a sparkle in her eye. One student commented, "She looked raring to go. She looked like she could take on the world."

A second way of giving support to success is to recognize the person's strengths. When you can make a genuine connection between a particular strength you have observed the person to have and its usefulness for being successful in the plan for action he has made, you increase the person's chances for success. You can name the strength and state how you think it will help him. You can remind him of ways he has succeeded with similar challenges in the past. Even in an initial conversation, you can name one or two strengths that you have seen evidence of in the conversation, and offer your recognition of these strengths and how they might be helpful for conducting the plan of action.

Make a Plan for Accountability

A good action plan includes arrangements for accountability. You can begin by making an appointment or other plan for your follow-up with the person. If this session is the first of two or three pastoral conversations, planning for follow-up is easy. You simply schedule the next session, giving enough time for the person to complete her plan, and not so much that the commitment can be lost in the shuffle of everyday life. Everyone's circumstances are different, but in general I find that a week or two is a good time frame.

You might consider having the person report back to you when he has completed one of the steps, such as sending you an email when he has made a phone call. Leave the responsibility with him to communicate with you. A guideline is that you do not want to be working harder than your parishioner. It is his life and his responsibility and his rewards or consequences for what he does or does not do.

If this is a one-time conversation, planning follow-up is not so clear-cut. It is important to follow up, however. Sharing successes and failures with another person helps people to take steps they have difficulty taking on their own behalf. I recommend setting a definite time and manner for the follow-up conversation. You might ask, "Will you send me an email on this date and let me know how it is going?" or "Will you call me when you have...?" or "Let's set a day and time for you to follow up with me."

You will need to decide how much responsibility you want to take if the person does not follow up. Some ministers put the dates on their calendars and follow up after a few days have elapsed from the agreed-upon time. Others assume that the responsibility for follow-up belongs with the parishioner. Still others make this decision based on their perception of the urgency, intensity, and seriousness of the problem. In general, I would lean toward leaving the responsibility with the person unless I have a good reason to do otherwise.

The primary issue you want to remember about accountability is that it is your goal to help the person to be accountable to herself and not to you. Even if she follows up with you, the goal is to assist her in being accountable to herself. You can also encourage help from other people. For example, you might ask, "Who in your life would be a good person to help you be accountable to yourself about following your plan?" When she names someone you can ask her, "When and where will you talk to that person about helping you?" Asking this question can help the minister avoid the problem of taking on too much responsibility for your congregant. You are responsible to her as you lead these ministry conversations and as you continue working as her minister. You are not responsible for her or what she does or does not do. You are responsible to her but not for her. Be careful not to assume responsibility that does not belong to you. Remember that doing so trespasses on another person's territory.

Finally, you can assist your congregant with accountability by simply asking, "How will you be accountable to yourself for following your plan?" This simple question helps him strengthen his commitment to his plan. I have heard a variety of answers to this question. Sometimes people say that checking it off their calendar or to-do list will be enough accountability for them. Others speak of creating charts, using gold stars, and offering themselves rewards. Sometimes people plan a definite time to review their progress, perhaps linking it to work they already do, such as planning their schedules or reviewing their calendars.

Conclude the Conversation

When you reach this point in step six, you are ready to conclude both the step and the conversation. You might conclude the step by offering a recap or statement of encouragement. "You have planned to do this...I see your gifts..." You might also say something like "I believe in you" or "You have made an important plan to accomplish something worthwhile. You have listened to your own wisdom, to God, and to other resources. May God be with you as you take action on the plan you have made a commitment to follow."

As you conclude the conversation as a whole, you might pray with the person if it seems appropriate. You might end with a time of connection that mirrors what you did in step one. For example, if you began with a time of silence and centering, you might conclude with a time of silence and centering. Just as you began with social conversation, it might be helpful to conclude the conversation with a brief social conversation. This process helps your congregant transition from exploring his life in depth to leaving your office, getting in the car, and going on with the day. I sometimes ask the person what he will be doing or where he will be going next. You can also say something to remind and assure the individual of your ongoing ministerial relationship with him. This statement can be as simple as "I'll see you at church on Sunday." You might say to the person, "I won't ask you about this topic in a pubic setting because I don't want to intrude, but I welcome your telling me how things are going." As you follow up with your congregant, or have follow-up sessions, notice if things do not improve or if the person has not taken the steps he chose and committed to take. You will want to consider if referral is necessary or would be useful for the person.

Pitfalls to Avoid

The primary pitfall to avoid at this step is believing that you are responsible for what the person chooses to do, that you are responsible for how good her action plan is, and that you have to make it happen. To reiterate an important point, you are responsible for leading the conversation and asking powerful questions. The person is responsible for searching for answers, accessing wisdom and resources, making the choice of an action plan, and following through with the plan. Do not get these responsibilities confused!

Sometimes we want people to be further along than they are in their journeys. This desire to get ahead of ourselves can be seen as one of the temptations Jesus faced. Turning stones into bread after a fast is to get several steps ahead of the process. According to Parker Palmer, it is customary to break a fast with water, or other liquids and soft foods. Bread is several steps away. You do not break a fast with bread. Palmer reflects, "When we rush to the aid of a fasting person, attempting to be 'relevant' by insisting that he or she eat, we are likely not only to be irrelevant but to do harm as well."[2] It can be tempting to ask the person to commit to more actions than she is ready to take. I have never known this question to be helpful. Have faith that when the person takes the step she is ready to take, then she will become prepared and equipped for the next steps.

You might also be tempted to do things for the other person. When you do things for someone that she can do for herself, you are hindering her growth toward love rather than helping it. Watch out for this tendency and avoid this pitfall. It is a temptation to trespass against another person.

Integrating Previous Steps and Ongoing Use of This Step

In this final step, you will be integrating all five of the previous ones. Some of the powerful questions you ask will also help the person maintain and make use of his connection to God, his own higher self, and other people. You will notice if the person loses this connection as you discuss the action plan he is willing to commit to do, and you will help him to get back on track with these connections. As you conduct step six, Generate Commitment to a Specific, Loving Action Plan, you will continue attending to how he will move from where he is to where he wants to be. As you are developing the person's action plan in step six, you will reference the realistic, focused goal you set for this conversation. Throughout this step you will also continue to invite help and improve the plan you began in step four. Finally, you will notice and address obstacles that surface. That might mean changing the plan in a quick way, or it might mean making arrangements to address another obstacle later. You do not have to be the one to address other obstacles, as there are other resources the person can access, but you might plan a future conversation. Pay attention to issues of stewardship and responsibility (what is yours and what is not) as you make this decision.

Since this is the final step, there will not be an ongoing use of it in this conversation. The plans for follow-up, however, do provide accountability for the commitments to the action plan your parishioner created. Your follow-up plan might be a brief discussion but not another CARING conversation. If in your follow-up discussion, he tells you that he did not do any of the actions he committed to do, you might ask, "What got in your way?" and "How can you get around that obstacle?" to give him another chance for success. You will need to decide if you want to offer a full CARING conversation or not, either immediately or scheduled for later. You will also need to decide if the situation calls for a referral. If he tells you he did follow the action plan, you can provide encouragement and support while hearing about what happened.

If your follow-up plan is to have a second CARING conversation with the person, then you simply follow the CARING process. Begin with a time of connection, then when you enter the second step, Attend to the Journey, you can start the "where you are" section by asking how her actions went. Sometimes the congregant might want to explore in this conversation whatever obstacles blocked her from following her plan. Other times, she has another goal for the conversation that seems more pressing. Either route can be helpful. You will agree upon an area of focus, and then follow the process of a CARING pastoral conversation.

How to Know You Have Completed This Step

When you have finished the following activities, you have accomplished this step.

- A plan of action has been generated and written down.

- You have asked for and received specifics.

- A plan for accountability is in place.

- The person may seem to feel complete, hopeful, and ready to take action.

- You may feel completion, peace, and neutrality.

- You have concluded the conversation with a plan for follow-up.

You have now reviewed all six steps of the CARING process. Read the conclusion for more suggestions about applying this material to your life and ministry.

CONCLUSION

We have journeyed a long way together. You have learned some skills for providing ministry. You have digested a process for inspiring people to change. And you have experienced a number of real-life examples through the reading and, I hope, in your own ministry as well.

Overview

In the introduction to this book, I offered to help you find solutions to several common problems ministers face. Now, here, in the conclusion, I would like to revisit those goals and summarize what this book has taught you about them. The first goal I described was to teach you how to move from floundering in your ministry conversations to having a reliable process that you can follow. The six-step CARING process is easy to remember and to follow. I have given you an order of questions and the topics to address within each step. It is a reliable process that you can follow without floundering that will create effective, meaningful pastoral conversations that lead to change and growth.

The second goal I described is to help you move from having unrealistic expectations to realistic expectations about your ministry conversations. You have learned that you face temptations similar to those Jesus faced as he was beginning his ministry. You now recognize the desire to be spectacular, relevant, and powerful as temptations.[1] You have adjusted your expectations to be authentic, realistic, and humble, helping people choose the changes they wish to make rather than telling them what to do. This change will bring more joy, and, paradoxically, more effectiveness to your ministry.

The third goal I set for this book was to assist you with journeying from struggling with demands on your time to practicing good stewardship of your time in ministry conversations. Having developed good skills and having learned the CARING process, you then practice making good decisions about how many sessions you offer to how many people. You base these decisions on the whole picture of your calling; your job description; and the limitations of time, energy, skill, and training. I have suggested that you work with any one person for no more than three to four sessions. This paves the way for her to receive more specialized help if she needs it and for you to be a good steward within the totality of your ministry. Following this practice will provide more freedom and time for you.

The fourth goal I described for this book was to help you travel from having difficulty in helping people master their fears, overcome their doubts, and navigate around their obstacles to possessing powerful skills and techniques to guide people to self-management, emotional growth, and spiritual progress. You have learned ways to help people hear the messages of their feelings and thoughts, assess and change their thoughts if necessary, and choose actions based on truth and love. You have also learned techniques to help people navigate around their obstacles, understand the messages of their emotions, change the thoughts that create problems, and grow spirituality toward Christlike love.

The fifth goal I set for this book was to help you move from uncertainty about what is your responsibility and what is your parishioner's responsibility in order that you might help people with more ease and effectiveness. I have given you a realistic vision for the responsibilities that are yours compared to the responsibilities that belong to your parishioners. Your responsibility is to guide the conversation; to ask powerful questions; to facilitate the person's connection with his own wisdom, God, and other resources; to support his development of an action plan; and to follow up with him afterward. Your congregant's responsibility is to be honest with you; to seek the answers to the powerful questions you ask; to connect with himself, other people, and God; to create an action plan; to commit to that action plan; and to take action. If you can embrace the ideas presented here, you will feel more freedom and joy in your ministry *and* your pastoral conversations will be more effective.

The final goal I established for this book was to help you travel from wanting more knowledge and skills for ministry conversations to having a reliable methodology and trustworthy techniques to consistently help your parishioners solve their problems and reach their goals. The skills and the steps of the CARING process will serve this purpose in your ministry if you practice them and develop your abilities. I hope that you are pleased with this contribution to your ongoing ministry.

I believe this model for pastoral conversations has much to offer all types of ministers as a format to assist people in making the changes they desire. It has the advantage of positioning the minister as helper and the congregant as expert and authority (author) of his life. The CARING process is beneficial because it is easy for beginning ministers to understand, remember, and apply. It can be done without extensive training. At the same time, this process will help experienced ministers be even more effective. The veteran minister will recognize steps that he is quite good at, and others that he could improve. Knowing and following the process will greatly enhance the important work of caring for the people with whom you minister.

Applications to Ministry

Having met these goals, I would like to offer some additional applications to ministry. The CARING process can be used in your ministry in ways that are not obvious at first glance. Preachers can be intentional about including all of the following skills in their sermons: displaying empathy; modeling compassion; demonstrating that he or she has listened well; responding; asking powerful questions; overcoming obstacles; helping people envision and plan a desired change; and asking for definite, specific commitments.

Other ministers, including ministers with youth or senior adults, music ministers, ministers of education, chaplains, and spiritual directors can make use of these techniques. I encourage you to creatively look for ways to include the skills and processes of effective pastoral conversations that you have learned here in other responsibilities of your ministry. You might find that you enjoy tasks that had previously been uncomfortable. Jobs that were previously difficult might become easier. For example, you can experiment with using this process to guide committee meetings. You might also teach it to members of your congregation to facilitate their ability to care for one another.

Finally, you might use the CARING process to guide your own growth and development. You could practice it as a spiritual discipline, perhaps along with journaling or prayer. To do so, use the six steps and guide yourself through the process. My students have reported that these six steps are a meaningful and useful process for connecting with God, with their own inner wisdom, and with other people; for solving problems; and for creating action plans. One student even mapped out her entire doctoral project using the CARING process as a guide. Another said that the CARING process was the most useful spiritual practice he had ever undertaken to receive guidance from God about his own needs and problems. An additional benefit of using the CARING process in your own life is that you will become more skilled at leading your parishioners through it.

Next Steps

I would now like to give you some guidance about the next steps of your journey to become a competent, effective, joyful guide of pastoral conversations. Practice the CARING process in your own life. You can use it as a journaling or prayer guide to help you work through your own problems. The more you use it with clarity and effectiveness in your own life, the better you will be at using it with your congregants.

You might also choose to practice it with another minister. A practice partner who is also reading and applying the principles in this book would be very helpful. I encourage the development of dyads or groups to develop your skill and experience in the CARING process.

You might also consider if there are family members and friends who would be good candidates with whom you might practice CARING conversations. If you do this exercise, make sure that the person knows what you are doing and is supportive of your working with her in this way. If the person can give you clear feedback about how she experiences the process, that would be helpful, but it is not essential.

When you begin using the CARING process with your congregants, it would be wise to begin with smaller problems. Seek help as you need it from classes, CPE, continuing education, peer support, and professional consultations. See my website if you are interested in CARING, coaching, spiritual direction, or consultation opportunities with me.

I want to offer you my encouragement and support as you begin using this process with your parishioners. Remember your own big why for learning to have more effective pastoral conversations. Remember your goals for working through this book. At the beginning, I asked you to write them down. If you did so, go back now and reread your goals, noticing which ones you feel that you have completed and which goals need some more attention. Do you need to reread a section of the book more carefully, think about something, get help, or seek training in a specific skill?

Also remember the big why of this book: helping your parishioners to love themselves, God, and other people more fully, effectively, and joyfully as you help them to solve their problems and reach their goals. Remember that you are learning and practicing these steps for a big important reason. Do not lose sight of this big goal in the midst of learning the details of the CARING process. It can be a little like learning to drive a car. At first you are so focused on all the details of how to steer, what to do with your feet, what to look for, how fast to go, when and how to brake, and so forth, that the journey can be stressful. When you have practiced and learned the process, it becomes second nature and you can focus on where you are going rather than the details of how you are going to get there.

My final word of encouragement to you is to notice the growth you experience as you practice the CARING process. I hope that you are growing in grace as you are more connected with God; growing in community as you are more connected to others; growing in integrity as you are more connected to yourself, especially to your higher self; and growing in love as you are loving God with all that you are and loving your neighbors as you love yourself. Go in peace, receiving love from God and CARING for yourself and your congregants.

NOTES

Preface

1. "Definition of Terms," *ACPE: The Standard for Spiritual Care & Education*, 2016, www. manula.com/manuals/acpe/acpe manuals/2016/en/topic/definition-of-terms.

Introduction

1. "About ICF," *International Coach Federation*, https://coach federation.org/about

2. Martha Beck, website, https://marthabeck.com/life-coach -training/?gclid=EAIaIQobChMIxdjD3Lae4wIVjoKzCh0T5Qg YEAAYASAAEgIhwvD_BwE, accessed April 17, 2018.

3. Martha Beck, *Steering by Starlight: Find Your Right Life, No Matter What!* (New York: Rodale, 2008), xi.

4. Beck, *Steering by Starlight*, xi.

5. Tilden Edwards, *Spiritual Director, Spiritual Companion: Guide to Tending the Soul* (Mahwah, NJ: Paulist, 2001), 2–4.

6. Coach U, Inc., *The Coach U Personal and Corporate Coach Training Handbook* (Hoboken, NJ: Wiley, 2005), 206.

7. Coach U, Inc., *The Coach U Personal and Corporate Coach Training Handbook*, 274.

1. Connect with God, Self, and Others

1. For a detailed discussion of these topics, see John Patton, *Pastoral Care: An Essential Guide* (Nashville: Abingdon Press, 2005); John Patton, *Pastoral Care in Context: An Introduction to*

Pastoral Care (Louisville: Westminster John Knox, 2005); Margaret Kornfeld, *Cultivating Wholeness: A Guide to Care and Counseling in Faith Communities* (New York: Continuum, 2005); and Carrie Doehring, *The Practice of Pastoral Care, Revised and Expanded Edition: A Postmodern Approach* (Louisville: Westminster John Knox, 2015).

2. Resources include David K. Switzer, *Pastoral Care Emergencies* (Minneapolis: Fortress, 2000); Kornfeld, *Cultivating Wholeness*; and John J. Gleason, ed., *The Pastoral Caregiver's Casebook: Ministry in Crises*, vol. 2, Pastoral Caregiver's Casebook Series (Valley Forge, PA: Judson, 2015).

3. Ministers who have been trained as pastoral counselors will share their appropriate credentials and policies. This book is not intended to address pastoral counseling or psychotherapy. Of course, if you do have this training, you will communicate with people how you will work with them. If you are a therapist as well as a minister, you might find the CARING process a valuable addition to your skill set when you are helping relatively healthy people reach goals.

4. Kornfeld, *Cultivating Wholeness*, 103.

5. Gretchen Rubin, "6 Tips for Battling Loneliness," *Forbes*, May 19, 2011, www.forbes.com/sites/gretchenrubin/2011/05/19/6-tips-for-battling-loneliness/#298962003730.

6. Switzer, *Pastoral Care Emergencies*, 179–82.

7. Switzer, *Pastoral Care Emergencies*, 185–89.

8. Kornfeld, *Cultivating Wholeness*, 91–113.

9. Kornfeld, *Cultivating Wholeness*, 110–12.

10. "The LORD God formed the human from the topsoil of the fertile land and blew life's breath into his nostrils. The human came to life" (Gen 2:7).

11. St. Teresa of Avila, *The Interior Castle* (Mahwah, NJ: Paulist, 1979), 36.

12. Richard Rohr, *Immortal Diamond: The Search for Our True Self* (Hoboken, NJ: Wiley, 2012), 23.

13. Rohr, *Immortal Diamond*, 23.

14. Rohr, *Immortal Diamond*, 24.

15. Christina Grof, *The Thirst for Wholeness: Attachment, Addiction, and the Spiritual Path* (New York: HarperCollins, 1994), 26.

16. The CEB translates this as "a sound. Thin. Quiet."

2. Attend to the Journey and Assess the Need

1. Stephen Covey, *The Seven Habits of Highly Effective People* (New York: Simon & Schuster, 1989), 240.

2. Covey, *The Seven Habits of Highly Effective People*, 240.

3. Covey, *The Seven Habits of Highly Effective People*, 241.

4. John Patton, *Pastor as Counselor: Wise Presence, Sacred Conversation* (Nashville: Abingdon Press, 2015), 29–30.

5. Brooke Castillo, *Self Coaching 101: Use Your Mind—Don't Let It Use You* (North Charleston, SC: Booksurge, 2009), 28.

6. Margaret Kornfeld, *Cultivating Wholeness: A Guide to Care and Counseling in Faith Communities* (New York: Continuum, 2005), 128.

7. Gretchen Rubin, "Feeling Lonely? Consider Trying These 7 Strategies," *Psychology Today*, November 7, 2013, www.psychology today.com/us/blog/the-happiness-project/201311/feeling-lonely -consider-trying-these-7-strategies.

8. Andrew Lester, *Anger: Discovering Your Spiritual Ally* (Louisville: Westminster John Knox, 2007), ix.

9. Karla McLaren, *The Language of Emotions: What Your Feelings Are Trying to Tell You* (Boulder, CO: Sounds True, 2010), 167.

10. McLaren, *The Language of Emotions*, 295.

11. Martha Beck, *Finding Your Own North Star: Claiming the Life You Were Meant to Live* (New York: Three Rivers, 2001), 174.

12. McLaren, *The Language of Emotions*, 249.

13. McLaren, *The Language of Emotions*, 235.

14. Henri Nouwen, "Three Temptations of a Christian Leader," *Christianity 9 to 5*, www.christianity9to5.org/three-temptations -of-a-christian-leader, accessed October 18, 2018. See also Henri Nouwen, *In the Name of Jesus: Reflections on Christian Leadership* (New York: Crossroad, 1989).

15. Parker J. Palmer, *The Active Life: A Spirituality of Work, Creativity, and Caring* (San Francisco: Harper and Row, 1990), 105.

16. Palmer, *The Active Life,* 115.

17. Nouwen, *In the Name of Jesus,* 25.

18. Nouwen, *In the Name of Jesus,* 49–51.

19. Nouwen, *In the Name of Jesus,* 71–73.

20. Wayne E. Oates, *The Christian Pastor,* 3rd ed. (Philadelphia: Westminster, 1982), 264.

21. Denise McLain Massey, "Pastoral Care for Women: Telling the Truth and Maintaining Boundaries," *Folio* 11, no. 2 (Fall 1993): 1.

3. Reach Clarity about the Realistic Focus for This Conversation

1. Coach U, Inc., *The Coach U Personal and Corporate Coach Training Handbook* (Hoboken, NJ: Wiley, 2005), 205.

2. James Loder, *The Transforming Moment* (San Francisco: Harper & Row, 1981), 31–32.

3. John Patton, *Pastor as Counselor: Wise Presence, Sacred Conversation* (Nashville: Abingdon Press, 2015), 29.

4. Brooke Castillo, *Self Coaching 101: Use Your Mind—Don't Let It Use You* (North Charleston, SC: Booksurge, 2009), 28.

5. Kevin Murdock, "Called: An Exploration of 'Vocational Coaching' at First Baptist Church of Griffin, GA" (DMin project thesis, McAfee School of Theology, 2015), 65–66.

6. Karla McLaren, *The Language of Emotions: What Your Feelings Are Trying to Tell You* (Boulder, CO: Sounds True, 2010), 167.

7. McLaren, *The Language of Emotions,* 249, 235.

8. McLaren, *The Language of Emotions,* 167.

4. Inspire the Development of a Loving Action Plan

1. James Loder, *The Transforming Moment* (San Francisco: Harper & Row, 1981), 31.

2. Loder, *Transforming Moment,* 32.

3. Loder, *Transforming Moment,* 32.

4. Loder, *Transforming Moment*, 33.

5. Coach U, Inc., *The Coach U Personal and Corporate Coach Training Handbook* (Hoboken, NJ: Wiley, 2005), 15.

6. Suzanne Goebel, *Introduction to Professional Coaching* (Woodstock, GA: The On Purpose Group, 2006), 42.

7. Goebel, *Introduction to Professional Coaching*, 42.

8. Even though I do not remember where I first encountered these questions, I am grateful for all of the teachers, writers, and supervisors who have contributed to my understanding of this topic.

9. Andrew Lester, *Anger: Discovering Your Spiritual Ally* (Louisville: Westminster John Knox, 2007), ix.

10. Karla McLaren, *The Language of Emotions: What Your Feelings Are Trying to Tell You* (Boulder, CO: Sounds True, 2010), 167.

11. McLaren, *The Language of Emotions*, 259.

12. Martha Beck, *Finding Your Own North Star: Claiming the Life You Were Meant to Live* (New York: Three Rivers, 2001), 174.

13. McLaren, *The Language of Emotions*, 249.

5. Navigate around Obstacles

1. Brooke Castillo, *Self Coaching 101: Use Your Mind—Don't Let It Use You* (North Charleston, SC: Booksurge, 2009), 28.

2. Castillo, *Self-Coaching 101*, 32.

3. Castillo, *Self-Coaching 101*, 32.

4. Castillo, *Self-Coaching 101*, 30–32.

5. Castillo, *Self-Coaching 101*, 32.

6. Andrew Lester, *Anger: Discovering Your Spiritual Ally* (Louisville: Westminster John Knox, 2007), ix.

7. Karla McLaren, *The Language of Emotions: What Your Feelings Are Trying to Tell You* (Boulder, CO: Sounds True, 2010), 167.

8. Martha Beck, *Finding Your Own North Star: Claiming the Life You Were Meant to Live* (New York: Three Rivers, 2001), 174.

9. McLaren, *The Language of Emotions*, 295.

10. Beck, *Finding Your Own North Star*, 174.

11. McLaren, *The Language of Emotions*, 235.

12. McLaren, *The Language of Emotions*, 249.

13. See also Denise McLain Massey, "A Word About: Praying When You Are Afraid (Phil 4:6-7)," *Review & Expositor* 115, no. 2 (May 2018): 267–69.

14. Beck, *Finding Your Own North Star*, 320–22.

15. Beck, *Finding Your Own North Star*, 321–22.

16. Beck, *Finding Your Own North Star*, 323.

17. Beck, *Finding Your Own North Star*, 322.

6. Generate Commitment to a Specific, Loving Action Plan

1. J. K. Rowling, *Harry Potter and the Sorcerer's Stone* (New York: Levine Books, 1997), 165.

2. Parker J. Palmer, *The Active Life: A Spirituality of Work, Creativity, and Caring* (San Francisco: Harper and Row, 1990), 107.

Conclusion

1. Henri Nouwen, *In the Name of Jesus: Reflections on Christian Leadership* (New York: Crossroad, 1989), 31, 51, 75.